101

MARKETING ESSENTIALS EVERY CAMP NEEDS TO KNOW

Jodi Rudick

american CAMP association

enriching lives, building tomorrows

ISBN-13: 978-1-58518-039-4
Library of Congress Control Number: 2007922383

Book layout: Bean Creek Studio
Cover design:

Coaches Choice
P.O. Box 1828
Monterey, CA 93942
www.coacheschoice.com

Dedication

This book is lovingly dedicated to Spencer, my very own happy camper. Thank you for picking me to be your Mom.

Acknowledgments

Marketers are nothing without feedback, advice, guidance, and suggestions. By definition, marketing is a profession dependent upon others. In my case, many, many others have contributed to my work for the past two decades—from the tens of thousands of people who have attended my workshops to the thousands of clients I have worked with on an ongoing basis. Because marketing is about constantly shifting perspective, I rely on just about everyone's opinion. Even my family, friends, and neighbors aren't immune from my endless curiosity.

I am also grateful to Andy Stein, who, for more than 13 years, has challenged me, both professionally and personally. Lastly, I must thank my mentors and entrepreneurial parents, Art and Chelle Rudick, who still teach me priceless lessons about business, balance, perseverance, and passion.

Contents

Essential #1: Pass the P's, Please
Essential #2: Talk the Talk
Essential #3: Review Marketing Plan Components
Essential #4: Inventory Your Products
Essential #5: Hook 'em, Reel 'em In, and Keep 'em Coming Back for More
Essential #6: Perfect Before You Promote
Marketing Assessment

Essential #7: Become the Architect of Your Future
Essential #8: Dream Big, See the Future
Essential #9: Align With Your Mission
Essential #10: Brand Yourself to Be the Best
Essential #11: Eliminate Idea Extinguishers
Essential #12: Release Your Inner Salesperson
Essential #13: Elevate Your Professional Esteem
Essential #14: Trust Your Intuition

Essential #15: Get Out of Your Head
Essential #16: Hypothesize Why They Buy
Essential #17: Interview Five Fans
Essential #18: Describe Me, Please
Essential #19: Solve Their Problems
Essential #20: Beg for Complaints
Essential #21: Tune in to Your Target
Essential #22: Engage in Child's Play
Essential #23: Widen Your Competitive View
Essential #24: Shop the Competition
Essential #25: Benchmark the Best of the Best
Essential #26: Shop the Shows

Preface

I was probably destined to write this book. As entrepreneurial 13-year-old girls, my neighbor, Joy Marschinke, and I decided to streamline our babysitting careers into a much more profitable joint venture. We realized that if we could pool all of our customers together and entertain them all at once we could make tons more money. (Keep in mind that the going rate for babysitting back then was a whopping 25 cents an hour.)

Joy and I took out our crayons and created a stack of beautiful flyers to promote our budding new business: "Joy and Jodi's Camp for Kids." We walked through our neighborhood and rang the doorbell at each home on our block, where all of our young prospects lived. Even back then we knew that the real decision-making power rested with the Moms and we made them an offer they couldn't refuse…

For a measly $5 we would take their kids off their hands each afternoon for an entire week, leaving them time to relax, run errands, and enjoy General Hospital without interruption. We even offered free door-to-door transportation via bikes, trikes, and wagons. We planned crafts, games, sporting events, and aquatics (if running through the sprinkler and playing in the rain qualify as aquatics.)

Needless to say, most of our prospects jumped at the chance to be part of our inaugural camp season. After a couple of days of cold calling and follow-up, our marketing and sales efforts paid off! More than 15 children came to our camp. All in all, it was a great success. But I do remember the rainy days being particularly challenging. While many of our campers wanted to return for a second session, Joy and I (and our Moms) were ready for a vacation of our own.

Even though our camp only lasted one season (by the next summer both Joy and I had discovered boys in a big way), I have never forgotten the experience. While things like technology and media have changed dramatically since the 1970s, many things have remained exactly the same. Kids still want and need to have face-to-face fun, and summer camp is still one of the best investments a parent and community can make in their children.

When it comes to marketing camps, I've worn almost every possible hat. I've been a camper, an employee, a parent, a donor, a sponsor, a consultant, a speaker and—if you count "Joy and Jodi's Camp for Kids"—an owner.

No matter what my perspective one thing has remained constant—I love camp!

Introduction

- I wish I could find a quick, easy way to attract more campers.
- I know my camp would be more successful if only…
- Who has time for sales and marketing? My staff is so small we barely have time to run our camp.
- I wish my community valued us more.
- I wonder why more people don't know about us.
- Things are so different today than when I was a kid! Who can compete with all this technology?

Have you ever caught yourself muttering any of the above phrases? If you have, you're not alone. Over the past decade, I have talked with thousands of recreation, parks, and camp professionals just like you. We discussed everything from budgets and staffing to public perception and technology. From these conversations one thing became very clear—you are very passionate about your camps and your campers! Unfortunately, many of you also told me that you lack the background, expertise, time, or money to effectively and competitively promote and market your camps.

As a marketing strategist, it is my job to help my clients reach more customers, generate revenue, and gain public support—with the least amount of time, energy, and financial expenditure.

This book contains 101 Essential ideas that will help you gain extensive marketing insight and confidence. But more importantly, each of the 101 Essentials is accompanied by an Essential Activity to move you to action. This book is not meant to teach you everything there is to know about marketing your camps. Instead, it highlights no- and low-cost methods almost anyone can master. Whether you read it from cover to cover or open to a random idea, one thing is certain: By implementing even one strategy in this book, you can make a difference in the way you communicate to your camp customers and prospects.

So what are you waiting for? Pick a page, choose an idea, and put it into action.

Marketing Basics

"Ads are the cave art of the twentieth century."
—Marshall McLuhan

Since the beginning of time, people have made and traded products and services. They have exchanged goods for services and skills for goods. While communication tools have come a long way since the first cave drawings, most marketing principles have remained intact. With some updates and enhancements to meet the unique needs of camps and their customers, this chapter explores the basic marketing essentials.

While communication methods have changed since prehistoric times, the overall goals have remained the same. People have a need to share ideas, feelings, information, and opinions with one another.

Essential #1: Pass the P's, Please

The "Four P's of Marketing"—price, product, place, and promotion—have long been at the core of marketing education. While the traditional model is best applied to product-based businesses, the tenets—with a little modification—are extremely useful for service businesses, nonprofit organizations, and even your camp.

However, at least four additional P's—perspective, planning, philosophy, and people—are also essential to modern marketing effectiveness. Together, these eight P's ensure a holistic approach to your marketing activities. This new model guarantees that, when evaluating your successes or failures, you examine more than your promotion. In other words, if your camps aren't filling up the way you'd hoped, the problem may not be your brochure, website, or ads. The problem may lie in one of the other P's. Your price may be too high (or too low), your location (or place) may be a deterrent, or your product quality may be at fault (Figure 1-1).

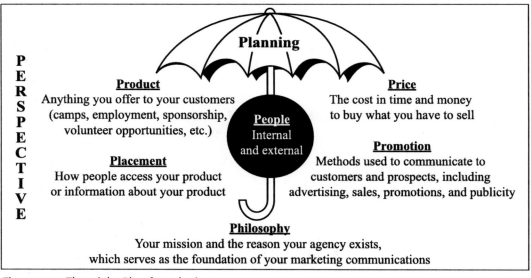

Figure 1-1. The eight P's of marketing

Essential Activity #1

What other P's can you list that might also impact your marketing and customer success?   Persistence,   patience,   _____ ,

_____ , _____ , _____ ,

_____ , _____ , _____ ,

_____ .

Essential #2: Talk the Talk

Most words have multiple meanings and applications. Communication, for example, can refer to everything from intimate, face-to-face conversation to broadcasting messages electronically.

Like all disciplines, the world of marketing has lots of jargon and terminology. Marketers also have unique definitions and perspectives for some common words. Because marketing texts often focus on the needs of mega-corporations, the following definitions have been reworked to better relate to the unique needs of camps and other recreation agencies:

■ *Marketing*—everything you do to get and keep your customers

■ *Product*—anything you sell or offer to your customer. Products do not have to be tangible. Common camp products include:

- Camp sessions
  - √ Overnight camps
  - √ Day camps
  - √ Single-day camps
- Specialty camps (e.g., family camp)
- Retail sales
- Facility rentals
- Volunteer opportunities
- Sponsorships
- Education

- Classes
- Athletic programs
- Art programs
- Donations

■ *Buy*—The process of exchanging resources, such as time or money, for the services or goods offered by another. Your customers don't always "buy" with money. Anytime anyone gives you their money or their time, they "buy" from you.

■ *Features*—characteristics of your "product"

■ *Personal or individual benefits*—what your service or product does for your direct customer or end-user

■ *Community or social benefits*—what your product does for the community at large

■ *Customer*—anyone you serve (internal or external)

■ *Staff*—anyone who serves your customers, paid or unpaid

■ *Front-line staff*—anyone who has direct contact with customers, on the phone, in person, in writing, or electronically (via email)

■ *Customer proximity*—The closer you are to the customer, the more power you *should* have in your organization. Managers serve front-line staff. A manager's job is to help front-line staff better serve customers. Remember, front-line staff members don't serve managers, they serve customers.

Essential Activity #2

Don't just breeze over these definitions. Reread each term and its definition and ask yourself:

- Do I agree with this definition?
- Does my behavior reflect my commitment to these marketing concepts?
  In other words, are you talking the talk but not walking the walk?

Essential #3: Review Marketing Plan Components

Marketing plans, like customers and camps, come in all shapes and sizes. Hundreds (maybe thousands) of books, seminars, computer programs, and consultants are available to help you develop a sophisticated marketing plan. But don't overcomplicate your marketing planning process. Most of your plan is rattling around in your head right this very minute. You just need to take the time to write it down. While you may need to gather some data or do a bit of research, developing even a rough plan will launch you into a more strategic and effective direction. Don't panic! The marketing essentials will guide you through all aspects of the marketing planning process. Seeing a simple planning template can often take the mystery (and fear) out of the marketing process (Figure 3-1).

Objectives • Internal objectives (staff) • External objectives	What you want to accomplish?			
Target Audiences • Internal (staff) • External (campers and customers)	**End Users** Those who directly use your products		**Gatekeepers** Those, who by the nature of their job or position, have the ability to influence large numbers of your end-user targets	
Budget	How much you will spend in both money and time to reach your objectives?			
Message	**End Users** What you will show, say, or display to motivate your direct users?		**Gatekeepers** What you will say or do to encourage word of mouth and referrals ?	
Marketing Vehicles/Distribution Media and tactics you will use to carry your message to your target audiences	**End Users**	**When?**	**Gatekeepers**	**When?**

Figure 3-1. Marketing plan components

Essential Activity #3

If your agency has a master plan, strategic plan, or other long-term planning document, take it off the shelf. If the plan includes sections related to marketing communications, public awareness, or customer service, review those sections. How important might it be to weave new marketing ideas in with those in the existing plan?

Essential #4: Inventory Your Products

Retailers take inventories to count how many of each item they have on their shelves and in their stockrooms. As a camp, you don't sell many physical products outside of your boutiques, concession stands, or gift shops, but you should still be aware of your current product inventory. As a service-based business, you have a different but equally important type of product inventory that answers the question, "What do we offer and to whom?" (Figure 4-1).

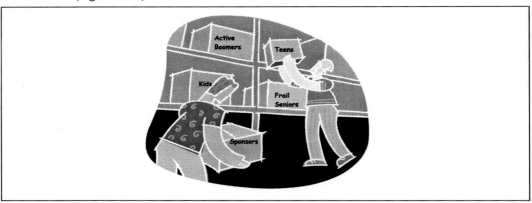

Figure 4-1. Organize products by target audience

If your camp is part of a large organization or park and recreation department you are more than likely segmented by product-based departments (aquatics, cultural arts, natural resources, parks maintenance, athletics, etc). If you are part of a national nonprofit organization, you may work within geographic segments. No matter what your organizational structure, you can become more customer-centered by taking inventory of your products based on target markets—youth, adults, boys, girls, families, teens, seniors, etc. You also may have noncamp products such as volunteerism, sponsorship, and facility rentals.

The product inventory template presented in Figure 4-2 combines season- and age-based criteria to segment products. Use this template or choose one that better serves your needs. List products as specifically as possible.

What do you offer for each target market?

	Children	Pre-Teens and Teens	Parents	Single Adults	Active Seniors	Frail Seniors
Winter						
Spring						
Summer						
Fall						

Figure 4-2. Product inventory template

Essential Activity #4

Complete the product inventory in Figure 4-2 or create one that better fits your organization.

- Review the inventory to ensure that your products align with your mission.

- Look for holes and opportunities to better serve members of your target audience.

Are your products out of date? Should they be refreshed to better meet the needs of your target audience?

Essential #5: Hook 'em, Reel 'em In, and Keep 'em Coming Back for More

Marketing, of course, is much more than advertising and promotion. It is not just about attracting customers and getting their money. Rather, marketing is about developing long-term customer relationships.

While good, creative, well-placed marketing materials are great, they are a waste of money and time if front-line staff aren't well-trained to handle incoming calls and customer questions. Furthermore, if your actual camp and activities don't live up to your promotional promises, your campers won't want to return. Worse than that, unhappy campers tell their friends and they won't want to participate either. Even with the flashiest website, the coolest MySpace account, and the slickest brochures, nothing makes up for bad word of mouth. The moral is: Strive for happy campers—every day, every session, every time. In other words, you've got to hook 'em, reel 'em in, and keep 'em coming back for more (Figure 5-1).

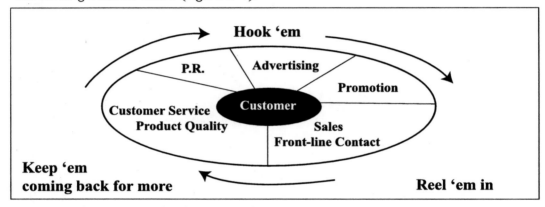

Figure 5-1. The customer development cycle

Essential Activity #5

Where do you fit in the customer development process? Do you work behind the scenes developing advertising and promotional tools? Perhaps you help staff the critical registration system on the phone or at a counter? Maybe you do it all, from designing the brochure and answering phones to teaching classes and coaching campers.

Don't be shy or humble. Grab a highlighter and highlight every part of the wheel in Figure 5 where you impact the customer experience. Share this model when training all levels of staff so that they, too, can see how marketing is everyone's business—even theirs!

Essential #6: Perfect Before You Promote

While perfection is something to strive for, everyone has room for improvement in one way or another. Major flaws, however, must be fixed before engaging in a full-blown marketing campaign.

It has been said that nothing destroys a mediocre company more quickly than superb marketing. In other words, the last thing you want to do is to attract new customers to check out your camps or try your services if you are still trying to work out a few kinks.

Imagine seeing a splashy ad for the grand opening of a brand new restaurant. You arrange the babysitter and drive through traffic across town to the restaurant, anticipating a fantastic evening of delicious food and lively atmosphere—as promised in the ad. Sadly, however, the evening is a huge disappointment! The food, when it finally arrives, is cold and tasteless; the service abominable, and the atmosphere chaotic and stressful. You (and your fellow diners) will never return to the restaurant. If only the restaurant's owners or management would have taken steps to provide a perfect "product" from the onset, they wouldn't have suffered such irreversible negative exposure.

Of course, things aren't as bad at your camp as they are at the restaurant grand opening! Maybe things are even perfect. If things *are* perfect, then you are ready to engage in a full-blown marketing campaign. More than likely, however, your organization or camp could benefit from a little improvement in the areas of delivery, responsiveness, customer service, quality control, or attitude.

The most important thing for a marketer is to have confidence in your people, product, and service. You could spend thousands of dollars and hours trying to build your business with flashy advertising and endless networking; but if the person that answers the phone is rude or apathetic, then all of your time, money, and efforts will go down the tubes. Countless businesses become disappointed, even furious, when their "marketing does not pay off." Marketing supports your existing product, company, or service. It will not camouflage your internal problems. Fix your internal imperfections and then forge ahead.

Essential Activity #6

The following marketing assessment will help you become aware of possible problem areas. It is a very simple self-evaluation that will identify your strengths and weaknesses.

Answer the questions objectively and honestly. Make sure you answer according to *the way things are* rather than *the way you want them to be*. Many of these areas will be discussed throughout this book. You may want to give the assessment to others in your organization, your customers, or your employees. You also will be able to use this assessment as a tool to measure your marketing progress.

Marketing Assessment

Date of Assessment: _____

The first step to creating your promotional strategy is to determine where you are in terms of your current customer and marketing resources, skills, and savvy. In other words, you must assess where you are so that you can know where you are going.

Instructions: For each category, circle the response that *best* fits yourself or your company the way it is *now*. Be honest! Record all of your answers at the end of the quiz.

Incoming Calls or Walk-in Customers

1. Incoming calls are always answered and customers are greeted by a friendly, caring person who has an extensive knowledge of all aspects of the organization.

2. Incoming calls or customers are sometimes answered by a friendly person, sometimes by an electronic device.

3. Our phones and employees are very busy. We just try to answer the phone before the caller hangs up.

4. Actually, we've had a very difficult time finding a receptionist or front-line person who can work our phone system. We should be filling the position soon.

Geographic Location (For Walk-in/Retail Businesses)

1. Our location is great. We get an ideal amount of traffic. We're right in the middle of everything. We are in a mall, retail, or business center that is booming.

2. Our location is good. We have some anchors around us that attract foot/vehicle traffic on a regular basis. Our business center is sporadically busy, depending upon the season and activities happening in the area.

3. We are somewhat off the beaten path. A few businesses are in our area that pull traffic occasionally. We don't rely on foot/vehicle traffic because it is limited.

4. Without a map it is almost impossible to find us. What little traffic we have is not of much use to our business.

Product Evaluation

1. We've worked very hard and have finally gotten all the bugs worked out. We're confident that our products/services/camps are the best available anywhere.

2. Things are definitely getting better. We are looking to make some changes soon and then everything should be fine.

3. We have had a lot of complaints lately. We are trying to address these issues, but it's so hard when you're trying to run the business.

4. We're not really sure what our product or service is. It's difficult to explain.

Competitive Analysis

1. Frankly, we have no competition. We're the only ones in our market area that offer our product or service.

2. Sure, we have competitors. We've done some comparison and feel our product/service is superior to anyone else around.

3. A handful of competitors are real thorns in our side. But other than these few "thorns," we don't run into competitors much.

4. Who has time to worry about the competition? We're focused on the day-to-day operations of our business.

Pricing Structure

1. We've really done our research and are positive that we are truly price competitive. We also have worked very hard to keep our prices as low as possible while still maintaining a healthy profit margin.

2. We feel that our customers get what they pay for. Our prices might be higher, but we make up for it in quality and service.

3. We try to get what we can and still make a little profit. After all, times are tough. We need all the business we can get.

4. Some of our customers have complained that our prices are a little high, but what do they expect? We have to make a buck, don't we?

Financial Resources

1. Cash flow couldn't be better. Now is a great time to look into investing in the future of this business.

2. Cash flow is okay, but I know it takes money to make money, so I am willing to allocate a budget to meet my marketing goals.

3. Business has been a little sluggish lately. I know marketing is important, but I really don't think I could come up with a budget right now.

4. Cash flow! What's that? We're lucky just to pay our bills every month.

Time and Energy Resources

1. I'm absolutely committed to spending time and energy on reaching my marketing goals! When do we start?

2. Even though I'm busier than ever, I'm convinced that I must make a concentrated effort to sell and market my business.

3. My intentions are good. I'll try to fit sales and marketing in between all my other duties.

4. Don't ask me to do one more thing. I'm fresh out of time and energy!

You and Your Team

1. I've never been happier with myself and/or my staff. We operate like champions alone and together.

2. Everyone has a few bad days, right? Overall, our attitude is pretty good. For the most part we are all committed to the success of the organization.

3. My attitude and company morale have been pretty low lately. We've had to let some people go and a lot of tension seems to be building.

4. We admit it. We're in the pits. No one seems to care about the future of the organization at all.

Your Customers/Clients

1. We feel like stars! Our customers praise us continually. We get many referrals from customers and alumni.

2. Once in a while we'll get a complaint, but we handle them well. On occasion we receive a letter of recommendation or a referral.

3. Our customer service could be a little better. It seems that we have to deal with more and more frustrated customers. Once we encounter a problem with a customer, they rarely come back.

4. If it wasn't for all these bills I would scrap my present customers and start from scratch. They are totally unappreciative and continuously complaining about one thing or another.

Awareness and Exposure

1. Everyone that matters has heard of our camps at some point in time. We've received extensive media exposure. Our name is everywhere. We are the talk of the town.

2. We've done a good job of infiltrating certain segments of our market. We've gotten some press and media exposure.

3. Our customers have heard of us, but beyond that we are pretty unknown. We mostly rely on personal contacts to create exposure.

4. Even our customers don't always recognize our camp or organization name. If we've received any press at all, it has been negative.

Response and Follow-up

1. Every lead, request, email and phone call is responded to immediately. No question is ever unanswered. If we say we will get back to you, we do it somehow—by mail, email, phone, fax, or personal contact. Our record-keeping is specifically set up so that nothing slips through the cracks.

2. Even in this hectic world, we have a good record of following up on customer and employee questions and requests. On occasion we hear of a situation where we dropped the ball.

3. It's almost impossible to follow up on every question, request, or contact we make. We do the best we can, but we always seem to be losing the names, numbers, or those little pieces of paper with the information.

4. If people really want the information badly enough they'll call or come back. Anyway, most of these requests and contacts are time wasters anyway.

Promotional and Advertising History

1. We have created award-winning advertising campaigns and promotional programs. They all work like magic to bring in more customers than we know what to do with. We are constantly getting comments on how nice our brochures and website look.

2. Our past promotional campaigns have been fairly successful. Some of them work and some of them don't. We'd really like to do something that gives us a better return on our investment. Our collateral material is nothing special.

3. Once in a while we'll buy an ad or something else from some salesperson peddling the latest promotional idea. It all feels like a big waste of money. We bought our letterhead at a quick printer or through the mail.

4. What promotional history?

Marketing Action Plan

1. We have a written marketing and advertising plan that was carefully created within the last six months after considering every aspect of the marketing mix. We wouldn't make a marketing decision without referring to this plan.

2. We did a plan a few years ago but we really don't use it all that much. We try to write down our goals as often as we think about it. *Or*, we have a plan that came from our headquarters that we refer to on occasion.

3. I pretty much have a plan in my head. I know which direction I want my business to go, but I just haven't found the time to write it down.

4. What exactly is a marketing plan? I make most of my marketing decisions as they come. If a salesperson calls about an ad or promotion I decide then. I'm never really sure if it's doing any good.

Your Communication Skills and Style

1. I love being around people. I have no problem meeting strangers or speaking in front of a group. My writing skills are strong and I think very quickly on my feet.

2. I like meeting new people and am confident when talking about my product or service. Writing comes fairly easy to me and I pride myself on being a good listener and like to help people with their problems.

3. I hate to mingle. I would much prefer to do behind-the-scenes work. I am much more information-oriented than people-oriented. I am able to write when I need to, but would much rather do research.

4. I don't make a very good first impression. I'm either excruciatingly shy or have been told that I'm loud and obnoxious. My written communication frequently has spelling errors and grammatical mistakes.

Record Answers Below:

Incoming Calls or Walk-in Customers   ____

Geographic Location   ____

Product Evaluation   ____

Competitive Evaluation   ____

Pricing Structure   ____

Distribution of Product/Service   ____

Financial Resources   ____

Time and Energy Resources   ____

You and Your Team   ____

Your Customers/Clients   ____

Awareness and Exposure   ____

Response and Follow-up   ____

Promotional and Advertising History   ____

Marketing Action Plan   ____

Your Communication Skills and Style   ____

What Your Scores Mean:

1 = Congratulations! You are a real pro in this area and a model for your industry. This category is a real marketing strength.

2 = You are doing well in this area. You have a good framework of knowledge and skills from which to build.

3 = Although your intentions may be good, you need help in this area. Fix it fast before big problems arise.

4 = Uh oh! This area is a major marketing weakness. Address this area immediately or it may cause your demise.

2

The Marketing Mindset

"Curiosity about life in all of its aspects, I think, is still the secret of great creative people."
—Leo Burnett

Marketing is not a department. Marketing is a mindset.

Marketing is the responsibility of everyone in your organization, as it refers to your ability to effectively connect to current and future customers. Thinking like a marketer is about becoming completely customer-centered and outwardly focused. Successful camps and billion-dollar corporations have one thing in common—they continually search for solutions, analyze needs, and arrange their "product mix" to best meet and exceed the ever-changing needs of their ever-changing customers.

Developing a marketing mindset requires that, no matter where you are in your camp's organizational structure, you accept responsibility for customer satisfaction. Rather than relying on past successes and reacting to customer demands, effective marketers have an attitude that is proactive and forward-thinking

The difference between mediocre and masterful marketing often lies in the preliminary planning. Your marketing plan, while simple, can be used to successfully manage your agency's growth and future.

Essential #7: Become the Architect of Your Future

Imagine you wanted to build a building that would stand for hundreds of years. Would you try to build your structure without a blueprint? Of course not! A blueprint—visual and tangible—is critical to ensure that each and every person involved with the project—from investors and administrators to contractors and designers—has a clear and consistent picture of the end result. The architect's job is to draw the future.

So, who is the architect of your future? You! Whether your job is to help build, create, develop, or maintain one tiny program or the entire organization, you truly are the architect of your future.

You are the architect of your future and your marketing plan is your blueprint.

Essential Activity #7

Find your inner artist and draw a picture of what you imagine your camp or organization will look like in 10 or 15 years. You don't have to be Rembrandt, Monet, or Picasso to create a masterpiece—Stick figures are fine. Use markers, crayons, colored pencils, paints, or any other media that helps you turn your abstract idea into a work of art. Keep your picture in front of you as you develop your marketing blueprint.

Essential #8: Dream Big, See the Future

Do you dream about the future of your camp or organization? Every successful organization and leader needs vision—the ability to see into the future on behalf of customers and campers who aren't even born yet. Do you have a clear picture in your mind's eye, or better yet on paper, of what your organization will look like in 10, 20, even 100 years?

What's in your future? Is it clear or is it fuzzy? The clearer your vision, the more likely it is to become reality.

Essential Activity #8

Just as you did in Essential Activity #7, pretend that you are looking into a crystal ball and it is 10 years into the future. Answer the following questions:

■ Will your camp or organization still be in existence?

- What indicators support your answer?
- What type of long-term planning has been completed?

■ Decades from now, what will your camp look like physically?

■ Will you have more or fewer facilities?

■ What types of campers or customers will you serve?

■ Will you serve more or fewer children and other campers than you do today?

■ Have you communicated this vision to your staff? How?

■ What strategies do you have in place to transform your dreams into reality?

Essential #9: Align With Your Mission

Almost every organization was created with a mission in mind. Whether your camp was developed by a single visionary or an entire group, it was likely established to fulfill a specific purpose. Businesses, nonprofits, and public agencies often formalize their aspirations by writing a mission statement.

Typically, a mission statement addresses the following questions:

- What "business" are you really in?
- What type of camp or "business" do you want to be?
- Who is your target market?
- What or who inspires you?

As you develop your marketing plans, it's important to review your organization's mission. Marketing activities must support, not conflict with, your mission. For example, if your camp was created to "help low-income children experience the joy of nature," you can't charge your campers more than they can afford. If your mission is to "support the environment by educating youth through outdoor educational experiences," you must be careful to choose marketing tools that are environmentally friendly, such as recycled paper, nontoxic inks, etc.

If you don't have a written mission statement, explore avenues to create one. Keep in mind that an effective mission statement is best developed with input from as many members of your organization as possible. Gather input via e-mail, mail, or phone, or during a special staff retreat or meeting. The best mission statement is relatively short—no more than three or four sentences long. A mission statement is not a place for you to brag or boast, but rather to declare your intentions as an organization.

Essential Activity #9

Find out if your organization has a mission statement. If not, create one. If you already have a mission statement, answer the following questions:

- Do you know what it is?
- Can you recite it by heart?
- Is it still relevant or does it need to be updated?
- Is it visibly posted or prominently included in marketing and communication tools? Is it part of your website?
- What will you do to better communicate your mission to staff, customers, and volunteers?

Essential #10: Brand Yourself to Be the Best

Your brand is more than your logo. It is the essence of who you are. Your brand allows people to connect emotionally to your organization's purpose. The name of your organization, camp, or product is part of your brand identity, too. Logos are symbols that help people recognize brands. Your logo should reflect your camp's personality and image. It should be simple and easy to reproduce. It shouldn't look like anyone else's logo.

Taglines, when attached to a company's logo, further communicate the overall benefit of the company. The best taglines have been in place for decades. Together, the logo and tagline communicate the USP, or unique selling proposition, of the organization. Your goal as a marketer is to create a strong and long-lasting brand identity. When people see your logo and tagline, you want them to instantly trust and believe in you and your camps. Your USP is like your DNA. It's what sets you apart from the competition. As a marketer, you never want to blend into the crowd. Your brand, when developed and nurtured, ensures consistency.

A great brand stands the test of time. Since 1964, the "smiley face" designed by Harvey Ball has been a universal symbol for happiness and pleasure. Mason City, Iowa, Parks and Recreation incorporated this timeless image into their logo with an inviting tagline that speaks to all.

Essential Activity #10

Log on to www.taglineguru.com. You will find many suggestions about what it takes to create a memorable tagline. You also will find a list of the "Top 100 Taglines."

- Do you use a tagline? If not, it's time to create one that helps others understand who you are.

- If you have a tagline, compare it to those on the list.

- Will your tagline stand the test of time?

- Does your tagline communicate your major benefit to your customers and prospects?

Essential #11: Eliminate Idea Extinguishers

Marketers rely on new ideas and innovation. Over time, people change, as does the world around them. As society, technology, and communities change, it's critical to not only embrace change, but also to fall in love with it.

It's not that past ideas have been wrong or ineffective. On the contrary, past strategies may have worked brilliantly in their day. But things change. Communication and technology have advanced beyond most people's wildest dreams. Children and youth have more options than ever when it comes to recreation, leisure, and how to spend their summer vacation. Cultural diversity has transformed homogeneous towns into mosaic communities.

How well do you adapt to change? Is your staff stuck in the muck of the past or eager to take creative risks and try something new? While your camp may have many timeless traditions, it's important to make sure your policies, programs, procedures, and systems still serve your customers well.

Your organization should reward creativity, innovation, and the willingness to try something new. Take the quiz in Figure 11-1 to assess whether you are a change champion or an obstacle to innovation.

While change can be difficult, create a culture that encourages new ideas. Sometimes alternate paths can lead to more rewarding destinations.

Place a check in the appropriate box to the right as you read through this list of comments, phrases, and nonverbal behaviors.

Verbal Extinguishers	Yikes! I know I've said this before.	I might have said this before.	I've never said this before.	Someone else has said this to me.
You can't fight city hall!				
They'd never go for it!				
What would people say?				
It's ahead of its time.				
Yes, but...				
It's more trouble than it's worth.				
No one has time for that!				
You're not experienced enough.				
People hate change!				
That would be an administrative nightmare!				
Because I'm the boss and I said so!				
You can't teach an old dog new tricks.				
Government shouldn't compete.				
Put it in writing.				
I'll get back to you.				
We'll send it to committee (or council or to the board).				
Do your research and get back to me.				
It's not in the budget.				
We have no budget.				
We don't have the personnel for that.				
This isn't your job.				
Leave it to the experts.				
No way would that work.				
I don't think so.				
This isn't a good time.				
That sounds like something a child would say.				
Maybe you need a vacation.				
If it ain't broke, don't fix it.				
The last person who suggested that no longer works here.				
Don't make waves.				
Don't rock the boat.				
Thanks. But no thanks.				
We tried that before.				
We don't know how to market.				
Marketing costs too much money.				
Now isn't the time.				

Figure 11-1. How open are you to new ideas?

Nonverbal Extinguishers	Yikes! I know I've done this before.	I might have done this before.	I've never done this before.	Someone else has done this to me.
Rolling the eyes				
Looking away				
Looking down				
Shaking your head				
Having a blank stare				
Taking or making phone calls				
Checking your pager				
Checking your watch				
Tapping your foot, fingers, pencil, or another item rhythmically				
Laughing uncontrollably				
Interrupting while someone is explaining an idea				
Pacing				
Going through email or papers				

Figure 11-1. How open are you to new ideas? (continued)

Essential Activity #11

After taking the quiz in Figure 11-1, answer the following questions:

• How honest and objective do you think you were as you went through the figure?

• How do you feel when someone gives negative feedback to your ideas?

• If given the opportunity, how do you think your staff would answer the questions about you?

• What will you do to open your mind to new ideas?

• What can you do if someone with a "but we've always done it that way" attitude gets in the way of your new marketing ideas?

• How can you make sure you are encouraging creative risk-taking?

Essential #12: Release Your Inner Salesperson

Selling is an integral part of every job—even yours. While you may not have a business card or job title that declares you a "salesperson," you sell ideas, programs, things, and yourself each and every day. Every member of your staff is part of your sales team, especially those on the front lines answering telephones or making face-to-face contact with campers. Selling is a critical part of the overall marketing process.

Even if the idea of "selling" conjures up images of pushy used car dealers in polyester suits and bad ties, remember that you are a salesperson, too. Great salespeople don't manipulate. The best salespeople in the world are passionate about helping others. They enthusiastically inform, educate, and share the *benefits* of their programs and camps with everyone they meet. Even people who are a bit shy can be very successful salespeople as they learn to listen and skillfully answer objections without sounding defensive. Superior salespeople know that follow-up—either verbal or written—is often required to close the deal. After all, your prospects are extremely busy and may need a little encouragement or motivation to complete the buying process.

Everyone is born with the ability to motivate others. As infants, people instinctively know how to get what they need. Their cries, wails, and coos inform parents to feed, bathe, burp, and hold them. As babies grow, so does their artillery of communication tools. They learn to use their fingers to point, their arms to reach, and a whole variety of pleasant and not-so-pleasant sounds to motivate a desired reaction. As toddlers, they learn that words, facial expressions, and tone encourage or discourage certain responses.

Babies instinctively know how to get the attention they need. As people grow, their communication repertoire gets more and more sophisticated. Through trial and error, people learn what motivates others and what doesn't.

Children quickly learn that their behavior has consequences and that words can be used to talk others into doing and buying all sorts of things. If you ever talked your parents into increasing your allowance, buying you a toy, sending you to camp, staying out past curfew, or letting you borrow the car, then you acted as a successful salesperson. In many cases, the sales skills you learned and relied on as a child have become part of your personal and professional success. In other cases, that natural salesperson may have been suppressed along the way.

If your inner salesperson has gone into hiding, it may be time to pick up a book about selling from your local library, bookstore, or online retailer. Sales gurus such as Tom Hopkins, Zig Ziglar, Brian Tracy, Spencer Johnson, and Jeffrey Gitomer have been sharing sales secrets for decades. If you're searching for sales solutions or confidence, you're clearly not alone. You may also want to investigate a course in selling or presentation skills. Your local chamber of commerce, community college, or American Camp Association chapter can typically lead you to the education you need. Organizations such as Toastmasters (www.toastmasters.org) can help you practice communication skills on a regular basis.

Essential Activity #12

Think about the last time you successfully sold something. It might have been an idea, sponsorship, or yourself when you landed your job. Your "customer" might have been your boss, staff, board, camper, parent, volunteer, or a businessperson.

• What part of the sales process was most difficult for you?

• Are you better at written or verbal selling?

• How well do you handle rejection?

• What can you do to overcome fears or anxieties associated with selling?

Essential #13: Elevate Your Professional Esteem

It's not always easy to be passionate and enthusiastic every minute of every day. Some of your work, while necessary, is downright boring or tedious. Some tasks required of you and your staff are laborious and difficult. Often the sheer volume of work can be frustrating. However, your attitude as a manager, leader, or counselor is contagious. Your staff, volunteers and campers take cues from you.

While self-esteem refers to the way a person sees himself, professional esteem refers to the way a person or team views the organization or camp. When professional esteem is high, you project a positive, appealing image. When professional esteem is low, the outward image comes across as uninviting or even unsafe. Not even the most innovative marketing can make up for poor professional esteem.

Anyone can have a bad day or wake up on the wrong side of the bunk. As a marketer, you must always remember that you are a representative of your organization and its quality. If you aren't happy, how can you expect your staff and customers to be happy? You must train your staff in such a way that they, too, know that they represent your camp—even when they are not at camp.

Even though you might like to change certain things about your camp, organization, leaders, or facilities because they are imperfect, it is never acceptable to vocalize complaints to customers. Instead, create an atmosphere where you encourage staff to share concerns with you and other camp leadership without fear. Be accessible, so that small issues don't blow up into major concerns.

Whether you score a perfect 10 or could use some improvement, the attitude you and your staff bring to your customers is integral to your marketing success.

Essential Activity #13

Answer the following questions to gain perspective into your organization's professional esteem. Ask staff members for input as well. Compare your answers with staff answers to gain perspective. If esteem is low, bring staff together to discuss issues and solutions before embarking on a full-blown marketing campaign. In other words, fix internal problems before introducing new prospects to your camp and staff.

On a scale of 1 to 10 (10 being the best), how would you rank the following?

- Staff attitude as a whole: _____

- Customer satisfaction: _____

- Your attitude as a whole: _____

- The hierarchy's acceptance of new ideas: _____

How is your organization's professional esteem?

- Are facilities well-maintained, safe, and clean?

- Are staff members willing to try new things and activities?

- Do staff members feel good about their work?

- Do staff members return year after year?

- Do they feel valued and appreciated?

- Do they take pride in their physical appearance?

- Do they demonstrate a commitment to the camp's overall quality?

Essential #14: Trust Your Intuition

Even if you are new to your camp or to the world of marketing, you have an incredible amount of intuitive insights into what it will take to better promote your programs and products. After all, you have been a consumer almost all of your life. With a little guidance, even the most novice marketer can offer valid ideas.

Throughout your life, you have developed innate abilities that allow you to understand yourself, your staff, your customers, and your environment. Don't discount your intuitive power!

Essential Activity #14

- Grab a timer and a pen and get ready to consider all aspects of the marketing plan. Before you begin:

- Set your timer to allow one minute for each set of questions in Figure 14-1.

- Don't overthink your answers and don't stop writing until 60 seconds are up.

- Upon completion, review your answers and highlight at least one idea in each section that you will implement in the next 21 days.

Clarify your product (What do you want to promote?)_____

Clarify your objective (What do you want to accomplish?) _____

Clarify your target audience (Who are you selling your product to?)_____

Minute	Component	Questions	Answers
1	Product	• What could we do right now to improve the quality of our products or services in the eyes of our customers? • What additional product or service would our customers most like us to offer?	
2	Price	• What could we do right away to cut costs without hurting our quality? • What offers could we afford to make to encourage new customers to try us or encourage current customers to be more loyal?	
3	Placement	• What could we do right now to help our customers or prospects better access our products or services? • What new approach could we try to reach different customers or reach current customers in a different way?	
4	Promotion	• What could we do right now to make our customer communications more clear and compelling? • What new ways of communicating with customers could we try right away?	
5	People	• What could we do to make our customers feel more enthusiastic and thankful toward us? • What could we do to increase our motivation and enthusiasm?	

Figure 14-1. The "give me five" marketing plan

3

Look Before You Leap—Gain Marketing Perspective

"The secret of business is to know something that nobody else knows."
—Aristotle Onassis

Before you embark on your marketing journey, you should do some preliminary research and investigation. This chapter walks you through some simple exercises that will help you redefine your camps for marketing success. By completing these very simple activities, you will gain better insight into your product from different perspectives. This research will be referred to again and again throughout this guidebook and will save you valuable time and money as you begin your marketing action plan.

Essential #15: Get Out of Your Head

What is your current business description? Right this minute you have a very definite perception of yourself and your business. The view in your head is perfectly clear. After all, you spend much of your waking life at work, in the office, at your camps, managing your camps, or talking about your camps.

Essential Activity #15

Throughout your life, at cocktail parties, networking events, in airplanes, and at the gym, you will be asked, "So, what do you do?" This question is probably the world's number one ice breaker. How do you typically describe yourself upon first meeting someone? This description is your one-dimensional, or flat, identity. It's how you see yourself.

Complete the following scenario as if you were introducing yourself to someone at a chamber of commerce mixer, conference, or anywhere where you might meet new people—nothing fancy and no cheating. Complete the exercise exactly how you would in a real situation.

You: "Hi, I'm _____."

The other person: "Hi _____. What do you do?"

You: "_____

_____."

How did you do with your self-introduction? Would your description stop your new contact in his tracks? Was it so intriguing that your contact wanted to hear more? Probably not.

People talk about their camps so often that they sometimes speak too quickly for people to understand what they have to say. Other times, they become so enveloped in their own perspective that they are unable to see it through another's eyes or ears. They tell people so often "what they do" that they often don't sound all that excited about it anymore. They tend to use jargon or abstract terms to describe what they do to people that they meet.

The trick is to get out of your head and get into the head of the person you are talking to. The next few essentials will guide you through activites and ideas to turn your flat description into one that will cause your listener to say, "Wow, tell me more!" or better yet, "Where do I sign up?"

Essential #16: Hypothesize Why They Buy

When it comes to your marketing, no one has a clearer perspective than your customers. Therefore, it makes good sense to talk to them to gather ideas and information before wasting time and money on marketing that might not work. Essential 17 will give you that chance. But good research always starts with a hypothesis, or prediction, of what that research will prove. Write your hypothesis before talking to customers. After completing your research, compare your hypothesis to your custormer's comments to see how in tune you are with your customers.

Your marketing research will help you maximize results and revenue. What do you think you will learn by talking to your customers?

Essential Activity #16

Take a minute to *guess* what three words or phrases your clients will use most frequently to describe you or your business. This activity is a great way to measure how in touch you are with your customers' perception.

Write down the three words you *think* will you hear most often:

- _____

- _____

- _____

Essential #17: Interview Five Fans

While market research comes in many forms, one of the simplest things you can do is interview your customers. Even by talking to just a few customers you can gain the objectivity necessary for making good marketing choices. By interviewing your best customers, you will capture important ideas about your strengths. This type of qualitative research, while simple, can help you stay customer-focused throughout your marketing planning process.

Who raves about your camps, programs, or business? By talking to your biggest fans, you gain valuable customer perspective that you can use to build more effective communication tools.

Essential Activity #17

Use the template presented in Figure 17-1 to interview at least five of your best customers. You may want to adapt the language based on the group you are interviewing. The questions could be asked verbally, personally handed to patrons, or sent via email, fax, or mail. Even a small number of responses will guide you in the right marketing direction.

These responses will be used in Essentials 18 - 21, so the sooner you complete your interviews the better you will be.

Essential Customer Interview Form

Name of camper/parent/company/client interviewed _____

Date of interview _____ Thank you note sent on what date? _____

(Send a note or token of appreciation to acknowledge each customer's time!)

USP (Unique Selling Proposition)

1. What *three* words or phrases would you use to describe me or my company to a third person?

A _____

B _____

C _____

2. If someone were to ask you why you do business with me, despite all of the other options available to you, what would you say?

_____

_____

Assessing Needs

3. What problems do you have that our camp/programs/activities/services help you solve or avoid? How do we (how do I, how does my staff, how does our camp) make your life or your child's life easier or better?

_____

_____

_____

4. What kind of problems might occur if our camp/organization/product or service was not available?

_____

_____

Quality

5. What problems have you experienced with our camps, staff, or organization? What could we do to better serve you?

_____

_____

_____

Gatekeepers and Influencers

6. Who influences you? Where do you go for advice? Who helps you make important decisions? Who do you ask for information regarding parks and recreation programs, health and fitness for your kids, family fun, reducing stress, etc.?

_____

_____

_____

_____

Choose Your Vehicles

7. Where else do you get information about the kinds of programs we offer? Please be as specific as possible.

_____

_____

_____

Figure 17-1. Essential Customer Interview Form

Essential #18: Describe Me, Please

In Question 1 of the Essential Customer Interview Form (Essential Activity 17), your customers were asked to share three descriptive words or phrases. Look back to the words or phrases you hypothesized in Essential Activity #16. How closely did the customers' answers match your hypothesis? If the words your customers used were synonymous with your predictions then you are in sync with your customers. If, however, your predictions were a bit off, this exercise has given you an indication that you may need to do a better job of getting into their heads and hearts. These words, while seemingly elementary, are great tools for marketing copywriters. They are the words you will use to build compelling headlines.

Essential Activity #18

After interviewing your five clients, transfer all of the descriptive words from Questions 1 and 2 of your customer interview forms into Figure 18-1.

- Which of the answers most surprised you?

- Which of the answers occurred multiple times or most often?

- How can you use these words and phrases to write better marketing copy?

Name of Client	Question 1: Three descriptive words or phrases	Question 2: Why do you do business with us?

Figure 18-1. Your clients' descriptions

Essential #19: Solve Their Problems

To succeed in the modern chaotic marketplace, it's no longer good enough to sell features. It's not even good enough to sell benefits anymore. To succeed, you must realize that your true purpose is to solve your customers' problems and help them avoid future problems. Questions 3 and 4 of your Essential Customer Interview Forms are directly linked to *positioning* and *solutions*. They also tap into *customer needs*, which lie at the heart of all great marketing messages.

In the late-1980s and 1990s (before most of your customers were born), it was unusual to even hear or read the word "problem" when discussing business. The edict of the time proclaimed "There are no problems. There are only challenges. You must look at problems as opportunities." While that last sentence is true, great marketing messages are built around the fact that you eliminate problems for your customers.

Brainstorm Questions 3 and 4 with your clients. Dig as deep as possible. The problem you solve might not be that evident anymore. After all, you might have solved the problem so well that your customers may have forgotten all about it. You could have eliminated the problem altogether.

For example, if you interview parents of your long-time campers, you will ask them, "What problems did your child have before coming to camp that camp helped them solve?" By asking or reworking the questions properly and probing a bit deeper, you might help the parent remember that prior to coming to camp four or five years ago her child was socially disconnected or complaining about summer boredom. Maybe your camp has given that child an appreciation of religion or spirituality that he never had before. Guide the discussion to get to the core of your solutions.

You might uncover some of the following problems:

- Lack of social skills
- Sibling rivalry
- Hectic schedules
- Bullying
- Boredom
- Self-esteem issues

- New to the community
- Financial stress
- Poor grades
- Stress
- Lack of time
- Lack of knowledge

When interviewing your customers, help them see below the surface to uncover deeper needs and problems affecting their lives.

Essential Activity #19

Questions 3 and 4 of the Essential Customer Interview Form ask your customers to list their problems, nightmares, inconveniences, hassles, and headaches. Transfer these responses into Figure 19-1 and review the entire list of responses:

• How well do you solve these problems for your customers?

• Were your customers aware of the types of problems you solve for them?

• Which of the answers occurred multiple times or most often?

• How will you use this information to write better marketing copy?

Name of Client	Problems	Solutions

Figure 19-1. Solving your customers' problems

Essential #20: Beg for Complaints

"Your most unhappy customers are your greatest source of learning."
—Bill Gates, Business @ The Speed of Thought

Question 5 of the customer interview form asks the following:

•   What problems have you experienced with our camps, staff, or organization?

•   How could we serve you better?

   Although your very best customers probably don't have lots of complaints, these questions give them permission to make a few suggestions that can help you improve your quality. Really encourage your customers to think about all of their experiences with your camps or larger organization. If you don't know what problems your customers or campers might have had, you will be unable to fix them. Plead with your best customers to think of any little thing that you might be able to improve. Commit to making necessary changes.

Whether over the phone, via email, or face-to-face, customer complaints are a form of marketing research. Learn to appreciate the customer who takes the time to tell you what you could do better. More than likely, they represent the feelings of other customers, too.

Essential Activity #20

Compile a list of the comments, suggestions, complaints, and ideas from Questions 5 of the customer interview forms. For each comment, determine what, if anything, you will do to make improvements in this area. Share the list with staff members who can directly and indirectly make improvements as well.

Essential #21: Tune in to Your Target

Your customers are the ultimate authority when it comes to your marketing. They can tell you who influences them and who they trust. They can tell you what to say and how to say it. The last part of the customer interview form gives your customers the chance to help you choose the best media to reach prospects just like them.

Regarding gatekeepers and influencers, customers will tell you who influences them and where they go for advice. This information will help you determine who you should reach to increase word-of-mouth marketing and referrals. The final question on the customer interview form is meant to uncover the best media options for your marketing plan.

As you know, you can reach your customers in countless ways. But, ultimately, the choice is theirs! Select media tools that are meaningful to them.

Essential Activity #21

Compile the ideas from Questions 6 and 7 of your Essential Customer Interview Forms.

- Were you surprised by the answers to these questions?

- Were you aware of the media outlets listed by your customers?

- How will you reach out to the types of people mentioned in Question 6 regarding gatekeepers and influencers?

- How can you learn more about the media and information resources listed in Question 7?

Essential #22: Engage in Child's Play

As mentioned in the introduction to this chapter, people sometimes become so imbedded in their own lives and businesses that they forget that others are not. Because marketing is based on communication, it is crucial that you are able to speak the language of not only your customer, but also of your prospect.

How would a prospect describe your business? For the most part, you should imagine that your prospects come from a place of ignorance about not only your camp, but also the benefits of going to camp altogether. Prospects are not dumb; they are simply unaware. Fancy jargon and acronyms will never impress a new prospect. Instead, they may intimidate, confuse, and create barriers.

To break through these barriers, you will want to test your marketing messages on objective communication geniuses—grade school children. Even if you are not trying to reach school-age children with your marketing, you must still be able to talk at their level. Children can help you get to the heart of your business and its benefits. If you can't explain your products, camps, or benefits to the average nine- or ten-year-old child, then you are probably not doing a very good job engaging a brand new prospect—no matter what their age.

Children have a unique and simple way of seeing the world—and your camps. Get their input to simplify your communication.

Essential Activity #22

Borrow a child from a friend, neighbor, or relative—with permission, of course! It's best if you don't work with your own kids, as they probably are too aware of your camp or business to be truly objective. You want to work with a child who has the fresh eye of the typical prospect.

Your job is to describe your "business" to this child in such a manner that he totally understands what it is that you do or sell. It's not good enough to say, "I run a camp." The goal is to break down your business into its simplest, most primitive form without specifically using the word "camp."

- Use charades, drawings, demonstrations, or pictures.

- Concentrate on verbs.

- The object of the exercise is to get the child to comprehend in such a way that he can clearly explain it back to you.

- Take notes and record comments and questions from your conversations with the child. Brilliance might be buried in one of his observations, inquiries, or challenges.

- After your conversation, use the insights to turn your flat, one-dimensional description (see Essential Activity #15) into a super-simple, super-brief description of no more than five to seven words.

- When people ask you what you do, you can respond in a way that is meaningful to a prospect and really causes them to say:

  - "Tell me more!"
  - "How do you do that?"
  - "Sign me up."

Essential #23: Widen Your Competitive View

You are much more than a camp. As you learned in previous activities, you are entertainment, stress relief, after-school care, a boredom eliminator, leadership training, and much more.

In addition, competition for your target audience's time and money is fierce. It's not just other camps who want to reach your customers. Malls, schools, television, the Internet, and other youth-enrichment programs are all trying to capture your prospects' attention—or steal your customers away from you!

When you expand your view, you expand opportunities.

Essential Activity #23

Make a list of your competition.

■ Begin with direct competitors who offer camps and other youth-enrichment programs.

■ Next, list indirect competitors that might offer products that meet the same needs as your camps but take very different forms. For example, if you are trying to reach preteens for your counselor-in-training (CIT) program, you'll want to list anyone who offers jobs or career-training programs.

■ Finally make a list of other places your target audience might spend their leisure or recreation time or money (the mall, watching TV, playing video games, hanging out on the streets, etc.)

■ Now that you have a list of your competition, make a commitment to learn more about them by:

•   Competitive shopping on-site or over the telephone (see Essential #24)

•   Get on their mailing lists.

•   Monitor the media looking for schedules, offers, messages, frequency, etc.

Essential #24: Shop the Competition

Just as it's essential to evaluate your own quality, products, strengths and weaknesses, it's equally critical to gain *marketplace perspective* by looking at how you stack up against your competition. You believe that you give the best service. You think your prices are competitive. You want to develop promotional materials that will stand out from the competition. But how much do you really know about them—in pure, objective knowledge, not just your assumptions?

Shop your wider competition. Where do your customers shop? Where do they hang out? Where do they spend their money?

The simplest way to research a competitor is to shop them via the telephone and in person, if appropriate. If you are in a service business, use their services. Your job is to find out what it feels like to be their customer. Does it feel better to be their customer than it would feel to be *your* customer?

While you may not have the time or money to engage in a full-blown competitive analysis, there are many ways to gather information about your marketplace that will help you with everything from pricing to recruiting. As a camp, you will want to pay particular attention to the following:

• The type, quality, and selection of camps, programs, and activities

• Schedules and session dates and times

• Costs

• Transportation

• Location

- Staff training

- Marketing techniques

In some instances, you may have friendly competitors who are more than happy to open themselves up to you. The idea is to find a benchmark within, or outside of, your industry for you to glean and learn from, not imitate and steal from.

Essential Activity #24

Use the competitive shopping form to gain valuable information about direct and indirect competitors (Figure 24-1). Remember the following:

- The more competitors you shop the better your perspective.

- The more often you shop the more current your perspective.

- Engage the assistance of some of your friends to help with your "shopping" efforts.

- Ask someone unknown to your staff to use the form to shop your organization.

- For superior objectivity, you may want to hire someone (or several people) to complete this task for you.

Competitive Shopping Form

Competitor name: _____ Date shopped: _____

Please comment on the following:

- Product quality _____

- Selection _____

- Pricing _____

- Customer service/responsiveness _____

- Employee attitude _____

- Delivery _____

- Location/accessibility _____

- Physical atmosphere/image _____

- Marketing materials _____

- Messages/offers/advertising _____

In addition, note the following:

Things that strike you (positively or negatively):

_____

_____

Things that they do better than you:

_____

_____

Things or systems that are customer-unfriendly:

_____

_____

The feeling you got while dealing with or "shopping" them:

_____

_____

How responsive did they seem to your needs?

_____

_____

If you were a customer, would you do business with them again? Why or why not?

_____

_____

Figure 24-1. Competitive shopping form

Essential #25: Benchmark the Best of the Best

Do you emulate those who are successful inside and outside your industry? *Benchmarking* is a process in which businesses research the most successful businesses in any given field to better understand their systems and processes. The ideas gained through benchmarking can often be applied to companies or organizations outside the field to improve everything from customer service to marketing success. Benchmarking, even in its simplest forms, can help your camp keep up with cutting-edge trends and ideas often reserved for large, well-funded corporations.

What can you learn by studying the best of the best?

Essential Activity #25

Dozens of books have been written about successful organizations such as Nordstrom, FedEx®, eBay®, Disney, Microsoft®, and Southwest Airlines.

- Log onto an online bookseller or visit your local library or bookstore's management or marketing section.

- Choose and read a book that pertains to a company you, as a customer, admire.

- Make a list of 10 ideas discussed in the book that you might apply to your own organization or camp.

Essential #26: Shop the Shows

What types of trade shows, community fairs, or expos might your target audience attend? Does your community host a summer camp extravaganza? Does it host a family expo, children's health and wellness fair, teen job fair, or some other event that brings your direct and indirect competitors together in one space? Trade shows are a great place to get an overview of your marketplace.

Even if you initially don't exhibit at these shows, you can use them as a one-stop opportunity to shop your competition. By walking through the types of trade shows aimed to attract your target audience, you can gather an incredible amount of information about everything from promotional techniques to marketplace trends. Trade shows are a great place to find out what's hot and what's not. Which booths draw crowds and which draw yawns? Just by watching your customers on the trade show floor you can see what products or services get them excited. You can listen for conversations that give insight into your target audience's needs, wants, and desires.

Trade shows, fairs, and expos offer a great, convenient place to shop lots of competition in a few hours.

Essential Activity #26

Find out what types of trade shows, fairs, special events, or expos are coming that will attract your target audience. Some good places to search include the following:

- Chamber of commerce

- Internet

- Media outlets that target your audience, and which sponsor or promote these types of events

- Direct or indirect competitors

- Members of your target audience

Put the events on your calendar and make it a priority to attend. Use your Competitive Shopping Form (Figure 24-1) as a guide to strategically gather information and new perspective on your customers, competition, and trends.

Essential #27: Seek Out Secondary Research

Primary research refers to data and information you gather yourself. When you talk to your customers and shop your competition you are conducting primary research. Secondary research, on the other hand, is research that has been gathered from outside sources. The information can come from the Internet, books, publications, radio, television, newspapers, and other media or reference sources.

Because primary research can be time-consuming and financially costly, good marketers always keep their eyes and ears open for secondary research that might impact their customers, products, competitors, or schedules. They also look and listen to the world around them, eagerly searching for trends that might help them better meet and exceed customer needs.

Essential Activity #27

Log on to your favorite Internet search engine. Type in the word "research" along with a description of your target audience (Baby Boomers, Generation X, Millenials, toddlers, science buffs, computer users, urban youth, Jewish children, Christian teens, active seniors, etc.). See what pops up and do some research.

In addition, visit the following websites:

- www.census.gov—The US census site is absolutely free, compliments of your federal tax dollar.

- www.acacamps/research—The American Camp Association links to articles and research studies addressing many camp-related issues.

- www.demographics.com—*American Demographics Magazine* hosts this amazing site, which addresses every possible consumer group and their buying behavior. The investment to access and search their extensive archives is minimal and includes a subscription to the magazine.

- Your library's website (or the library itself)—Many library systems subscribe to very expensive databases and reference services on behalf of their patrons. Make an appointment with your research librarian, who will be thrilled to educate you about the research resources at your fingertips.

Essential #28: Become a Trend Trekker

Trends help you understand consumer behavior, changes in sociology, the marketplace, and your customers. Consider the following examples of major trends and how they impact your camp:

- Technology has dramatically changed the way people communicate in business and for pleasure. Your camp's website, which probably didn't exist a few years ago, is more than likely your number one marketing tool.

- The aging population is a trend that causes many camps to add new programs and products to their mix that better target baby boomers.

- Culturally diverse populations and growing immigrant populations require marketers to diversify images and languages used in promotional materials.

- *Leave it to Beaver*'s nuclear family is no longer the rule, but the exception. Families come in more varieties than Beaver could have imagined. Your campers come from all types of family situations—single parents, three and four generations under one roof, and two-mother and two-father families. This changing family structure may require you to rethink how, when, and where you communicate with customers.

Essential Activity #28

Where do you look for these trends? Trends are all around you in the form of news stories, articles, opinions, statistics, surveys, research, comments, feedback, and even customer complaints. Use the step-by-step system presented in Figure 28-1 to make "trend trekking" part of your organization's culture and routine.

Step 1: Spot trend cues	Watch, listen, and overhear articles, news stories, conversations, speeches, comments, or even customer complaints.
Step 2: Capture information	Create a system to warehouse and file trend information. Use a box, file folder, notebook, or journal—whatever works for you.
Step 3: Brainstorm	Meet with staff, commissioners, volunteers, customers, your family, or friends to brainstorm ways that trend information might impact your patrons or the community.
Step 4: Apply	As you develop or enhance operations, programs, services, or facilities, retrieve and apply trend information.

Figure 28-1. Trend trekking

4

Develop Your Marketing Plan Foundation

"Good plans shape good decisions. That's why good planning helps to make elusive dreams come true."

—Lester R. Bittel, The Nine Master
Keys of Management

Like a building, your organization needs a strong and sturdy foundation to stand the test of time. The marketing planning process helps you create a customer-centered foundation. After considering each facet of the marketing plan as presented in this chapter, you are sure to create a highly effective marketing campaign. But, before you explore media, tools, or tactics you must first clarify your objective, target audience, budget, and timeline.

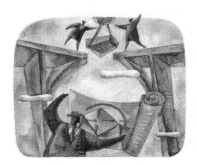

Essential #29: Permission Granted to Pick One Product

As you learned in Chapter 1, it's not only exciting, but also necessary to visualize your camp's future 10 or 20 years down the road. While your vision is a long-term picture of where your camp is going, your marketing plan is a short-term document—usually projecting 12 to 18 months into the future.

A marketing plan is also different from a master plan, as it outlines step-by-step strategies to reach your short-term goals. Rather than setting out to build a huge skyscraper of a plan, focus in on something a bit more manageable.

What is your overall area of responsibility? If you're like most camp professionals, you are responsible for many products. You may be directly or indirectly involved in many programs offered by your agency—camps, youth activities, fitness programs, facilities, arts and culture, retail sales, and staff development. You might even be a one-person operation.

As a marketer, however, it's important to give yourself permission to start with something smaller as you embark on your journey. You can always tackle the bigger projects such as community awareness, million-dollar sponsorships, and global brand awareness later.

Pick one specific product rather than trying to market your entire organization.

Essential Activity #29

Choose and write down the name of one specific program, event, facility, activity, camp, or service that you would like to market more effectively—an open house, family camp, volunteer opportunity, teen soccer camp, preschool day camps, equestrian camp for children with disabilities, off-season facility rentals, after-school camp, etc. Complete the following sentence:

The product I will create a marketing plan for is _____.

Essential #30: Know Where You Are, Know Where You're Going

Once you know what specific product or program you are marketing (see Essential Activity #29), you are ready to create a preliminary marketing plan beginning with setting your objective. Establishing marketing objectives early in your planning process can save you hours of frustration and confusion. Distinct from your mission, marketing objectives are often incremental steps to the long-term goals established in Chapter 2.

Marketing objectives must be:

- Realistic
- Measurable
- Attainable in a specific time period (typically six to 18 months)

Without a clear and tangible objective, you may feel like you are running on a treadmill—toiling, working, and sweating without really getting anywhere. But before you can determine where you want to go (your objective) take a minute to clarify where you are.

Your marketing objective is like the finish line of your marketing plan.

Consider the following examples of marketing plan starting points and their accompanying ending points:

- *Product: Preschool Summer Day Camp*
  Starting point: Last year a total of 400 children registered for Preschool Summer Day Camp. Eighty children registered for multiple sessions and 320 registered for single sessions.
  Ending point: This year you would like to maintain the number of children served but increase the number of multiple-session customers by 50 percent, from 80 repeat customers to 120 repeat customers.

- *Product: Transportation and Bus Sponsorships*
  Starting point: Last year you generated $20,000 to offset transportation costs.
  Ending point: This year you would like to double that to $40,000.

- *Product: Volunteers for Residential Camps*
  Starting point: Last year you had 100 volunteers who contributed an average of 40 hours to your organization (4000 volunteer hours).
  Ending point: This year you'd like to increase your volunteer base by 20 percent, or 20 people. You'd also like to increase the average number of hours each volunteer donates from 40 to 50. Overall, you would create a 50 percent increase in volunteer hours (6000).

If you are marketing a new program, your starting point is a bit trickier. Your objective won't be based on last year's or last session's numbers. You will need to choose objectives based on revenue recovery or profit motive, or by looking at similar programs.

Essential Activity #30

Where are you? Clarify your starting point in terms of the product you chose in Essential Activity #29. If the product is a repeating program, what quantifiers will you use to measure your success from previous years or seasons—how many participants, how much money, how many attendees, how many volunteers hours?

Essential #31: Prioritize External Objectives—
Where Do You Want to Go?

Most marketing objectives are externally focused, aiming to influence those traditional or end-user customers outside your organization, such as children, parents, sponsors, and donors. But as you'll see in Essential #32, objectives can also focus on internal audiences such as staff members, volunteers, or board members.

Essential Activity #31

Use Figure 31-1 to begin determining which *external goals* are most important to your agency. Add your own or adapt the ones listed.

Objective	Rank This Objective 1. Boiling—Should have been done yesterday 2. Hot—Should be done as soon as possible 3. Warm—Important, but it can wait 4. Cold—Not very important or pressing
Increase camp, program, or event participation	
Show thanks and goodwill to advocates and allies	
Convince the community-at-large about the vital importance of camps	
Create program or promotional partnerships with other camps, youth service organizations, or agencies	
Strengthen or expand the scope of relationships with current partners	
Recruit quality staff	
Recruit volunteers	
Increase facility rentals	
Increase participation of revenue-generating programs	
Increase concession and retail sales	
Raise donations and funds for camp programs and services	
Increase sponsorships and other financial support of camps from business owners	
Increase concession or retail sales	
Protect or increase budget allocation	

Figure 31-1. Organize your external goals

Essential #32: Marketing From the Inside Out—
Set Internal Objectives

Most of your marketing efforts will concentrate on prospective campers, their parents, or other external customers. However, you should never overlook *internal audiences* when developing your marketing plan. Internal audiences such as staff, volunteers, and board members can make or break your ability to reach marketing goals, since they have day-to-day contact with customers. Make sure they understand and buy into your plans before you share them with the public.

Internal customers are extremely important to your camp's success. The term "internal customer" refers to anyone who directly or indirectly serves your customers. Every member of your staff is part of your internal customer base. Often, depending upon their access to end-user customers, your board members, volunteers, and financial supporters may be internal customers, as well. Address the needs of internal customers and they will better serve external customers.

Essential Activity #32

Use Figure 32-1 to begin determining which *internal goals* are most important to your agency. Add your own or adapt the ones listed.

Objective	Rank This Objective 1. Boiling—Should have been done yesterday 2. Hot—Should be done as soon as possible 3. Warm—Important, but it can wait 4. Cold—Not very important or pressing
Educate staff about the value of our camps, programs, and products	
Improve customer service	
Increase value for our camps in the minds of city council/board members/other community leaders	
Energize and boost morale of staff and volunteers	
Re-energize and motivate our board of directors or other decision-makers	
Ease stress due to change within the department or agency	
Encourage ongoing networking efforts by staff and board members	
Reduce absenteeism	
Reduce employee turnover	

Figure 32-1. Organize your internal goals

Essential #33: Don't Go it Alone— No Marketer Is an Island

Although you may be well-equipped to prioritize both your internal and external objectives using your experience and intuition, rarely should one person create marketing objectives without input from others. Invite or request ideas and clarification from staff, managers, commissioners, volunteers, or board members to ensure that your objectives move you in the right direction.

In addition, creating and communicating your objectives to staff will help with everything from customer service to morale. By including staff in the marketing process, you create a sense of ownership and accountability.

One way to get input from remote off-season staff is to use a simple written survey. Not only will the survey help staff understand your commitment to strategic marketing, but it also sends a strong message that their opinions are important and valuable.

Essential Activity #33

After reviewing the sample survey presented in Figure 33-1, make necessary edits or enhancements. Then send the survey to query your staff, volunteers, managers, and commissions about their marketing expectations.

Hello Staff! We need your help!

We're excited to be developing a strategic marketing plan for our camps, but we can't do it without you! Please take 10 minutes to complete this survey. Your answers will help us establish goals and objectives to create the best camp experience possible for you and our campers.

Rate the following on a scale of 1 to 10 (10 being the best):

1. Staff attitude as a whole: _____

2. Customer satisfaction: _____

3. Your attitude as a whole: _____

4. The hierarchy's acceptance of new ideas: _____

5. Clarify for me what "products" or programs you work with or are responsible for marketing (e.g., day camps, overnight camps, special events)?

_____

_____

6. Which marketing objectives are most important to you? What do you want to accomplish as a result of upcoming marketing opportunities? Please rate the following marketing objectives on a scale of 1 to 4 (4 being the most important; write N/A if you feel it does not apply):

_____ Develop new ideas for future programs or camps (program/product development)
_____ Get more new customers to come to existing programs
_____ Gain greater "buy-in" from front=line staff for the marketing and sales process
_____ Gain more involvement/sponsorship from the business community
_____ Improve overall customer service from the customer's perspective
_____ Improve customer feedback systems
_____ Communicate customer service expectations to all staff
_____ Generate more "repeat business" from current (or past) customers
_____ Increase general awareness of your department and its programs
_____ Increase volunteer base
_____ Increase facility rentals
_____ Recruit, hire, and train effective staff
_____ Improve interdepartmental communication and team-building
_____ Create a department marketing plan and timeline
_____ Create new/improved promotional tools (flyers, brochures, direct mail, etc.)
_____ Improve positive publicity and media relationships
_____ Learn how to better handle conflict resolution

Go back and circle the three most important objectives on that list.

Do you have any other comments or questions at this time?

_____

_____

Thanks for your prompt response! We look forward to sharing our marketing strategies with you as they are developed.

Figure 33-1. Sample staff input survey

Essential #34: Create Micromarketing Objectives— Stepping Stones to the Ultimate Goal

Now that you have considered which marketing objectives are most important to you and your staff, you might be feeling a bit overwhelmed by their grand scale. For example:

- You may ultimately want to generate millions of dollars in sponsorships to build another facility.

- You may want to double or triple revenues from off-season rentals.

- You may want to increase the number of day campers by 50 percent.

These objectives are all admirable. However, they might feel a bit lofty or even overwhelming. Don't panic! One way to manage a large objective is to break it apart into smaller micro-objectives that ultimately lead you to your grand goal.

It's also important to understand that for most parents, choosing a camp for a child is a complex process and definitely not an impulsive decision. Parents and children must research, explore, make comparisons, and weigh cost factors before deciding to register. By understanding the "steps to the buy" that your customers ascend, you can chunk your marketing into easier-to-swallow activities.

Use stepping stones or micro objectives along the way to get to your ultimate marketing destination.

Consider the following example: Your macro-objective is to recruit 100 new campers to your aquatics camp.

- Your first micro-objective is to hold an open house for new campers to introduce them to the many benefits of your camps. The product you are marketing is the open house.

- Your objective is to attract 400 prospective campers to the open house.

- You develop a plan specifically designed to draw traffic to the open house and are thrilled when 500 prospects attend.

- You have exceeded your first objective and can move into the next phase of your plan, which is to transform open house attendees into registered campers.

- You have to get those excited prospects to actually register for the camp. Your next objective is to "close" 30 percent of all prospects who came to your open house with a marketing plan that focuses on follow-up, early bird incentives, referral rewards, etc. You may eventually have a third plan that focuses your marketing energy on repeat business and retention.

By reaching one marketing objective, you add a building block to your foundation. One marketing objective often leads to the next.

Essential Activity #34

Write down your macro-objective. Answer the following questions:

- What steps do customers take when making the decision to "buy" or "not buy" my product?

- How will I lead customers through the "steps to the buy"?

Essential #35: Write it Down and Set a Date

To be effective, marketing objectives must be measurable, realistic, and attainable in a specific time period (usually six to 18 months.) In other words, don't bite off more than you or your staff can chew with limited time and financial resources. If you have little or no marketing budget, you will have to take that fact into consideration as you develop your timeline.

Keep in mind that some objectives overlap and will cause multiple outcomes. For example, if you create a plan to increase donations for your teen camps with press releases and direct mail to community leaders, you may also gain public support and improve community awareness for your overall organization. This increased awareness may lead to greater teen participation, as well as more volunteer interest.

Essential Activity #35

Use Figure 35-1 to capture, combine, and prioritize your internal and external objectives. Make sure each objective is measurable, attainable in a specific period of time, and realistic.

Objective (Good)	Measurement (Better)	By When (Best)	Reality Check and Conditions: Is this goal realistic in the time allotted? What are the stipulations?
Sample Objectives			
Increase sponsorship revenue	Increase sponsorship revenue by 10 percent	Increase sponsorship revenue by 10 percent by March 15	Yes, with increased up-front investment and dedicated staff
Increase attendance at the Grown-up and Me Day Camp	Increase Grown-up and Me early bird registration by 20 percent	Increase Grown-up and Me Day Camp registration by April 1	Yes, with the new online registration system and earlier marketing
Decrease staff turnover	Decrease staff turnover by 20 percent	Decrease staff turnover by 20 percent for summer season	Yes, with better training, more strategic hiring, and incentive programs
Your Objectives			

Figure 35-1. Defining your objectives

Essential #36: Aim for the Target

At first glance, your target audience seems obvious. You want to reach campers, of course. But as you've learned, your marketing plan can help you reach many types of objectives. Campers, parents, volunteers, sponsors, staff, board members, and donors may all be at the heart of your marketing.

To maximize your marketing investment, it's critical to determine which types of people most want or need what you have to offer. Even with the biggest dreams, facilities, and budget, it would be impossible to be all things to all people. Different camps attract diverse audiences who are motivated and interested in many, many different features and benefits. The more you can zero in on exactly who your target audience is, the more you will be able to create a message and choose media that will grab their attention.

Different messages will attract totally different people to the same products or service. For example, parents love hearing that your camps are safe and secure. Teens might actually be turned off by a message that promotes safety. Instead, teens want to know that your camps offer excitement, freedom, and the opposite sex.

The more specific your target audiences, the more efficient your marketing.

To get the most mileage from your marketing vehicles, choose efficient targets. Because you can't be all things to all people, create programs and marketing materials that are targeted to specific members of your population. Consider these two types of marketing targets:

- End users—Those people who *actually* use your services, visit your facilities, participate in programs, attend your events, walk on your trails, play on the playgrounds, etc.

- Gatekeepers—Your secret sales force! These people and groups of people can lead you to multiple end-users. For example, a teacher is a gatekeeper who can help you reach children. Faith-based camps can look to youth group leaders at churches, synagogues, and other religious organizations. Sports camps can partner with athletic organizations, park and recreation departments, fitness centers, and gym teachers. Never approach these organizations as competitors, even if they offer camps similar to yours. Rather, approach gatekeepers as complementary partners who can help you meet the needs of kids who might not fit their target audience.

Two other targets should always be included in your marketing plans:

- Decision-makers—Those people who directly make decisions regarding your programs, services, budgets, funding, etc. (e.g., voters, city council, funders, board members, politicians)

- Media—Like it or not, most Americans make decisions based on what they see, hear, and read in the media. You can harness the power of the press to reach anyone in your target audience.

Essential Activity #36

Because your preliminary plan will focus on one specific product and one specific objective, it's your responsibility to aim your marketing at the most efficient target audience. As you develop your marketing plan, you want to clarify who in your pool of prospects best fits the profile of your ideal target customer.

- Who do *you* need to reach to achieve your objective from Essential Activity #15?

- Who needs you to reach them to access benefit-laden products? This question is especially important for nonprofit and public agencies. Review your mission statement!

Essential #37: Open the Flood Gates to Reach Your Target

Eighty percent of all "buying decisions" are based on word-of-mouth advertising. When choosing a camp, kids talk to other kids, youth group leaders, teachers, and coaches. Parents talk to friends, neighbors, health-care professionals, clergy, and complete strangers. When developing your marketing plan, make sure that you not only target end-users, but also those people who are in the powerful position to influence end-users. One strategically placed gatekeeper can lead you to hundreds of prospective campers and lead hundreds of campers to your door.

Essential Activity #37

Review the following list of gatekeepers highlighting those who are most important to your agency. Add any other gatekeepers that are important to your camp. Keep these questions in mind as you work through the list.

- Which groups can help you reach your objectives?

- Which groups could become obstacles between you and your objectives?

- Don't forget to include gatekeepers who can help you quickly spread the word.

- Use different colored highlighters to prioritize target audience members.

Common Gatekeepers for Camps

- Policy-makers and politicians

- Public recreation agencies

- Business leaders

- Educators

  - School counselors
  - School nurses
  - Principals
  - Teachers
  - PTA/PTO

- Police and law enforcement

- For-profit recreation facilities

  - Sports clubs
  - Health clubs
  - Golf courses
  - Country clubs
  - Martial arts studios
  - Tennis clubs
  - Skating rinks
  - Bowling alleys

- Recreation retailers
  - Art supply stores
  - Sporting goods stores
- Recreation manufacturers
  - Athletic shoe and apparel manufacturers
  - Equipment suppliers
- Private-sector health-care agencies
  - Hospitals
  - Clinics
  - Doctors
  - Chiropractors
  - Nurses
  - Holistic medical practitioners
  - School nurses
  - Mental health agencies
- Conventions and tourism
  - Meeting planners
  - Convention and visitors bureaus
  - Hotels, motels, and resorts
  - Activity directors at apartment complexes, mobile home parks, or assisted living facilities
- Trade and professional associations
- Women's organizations
- Children's nonprofit and social service agencies
  - YMCA/YWCA
  - Boys and Girls Clubs
  - Big Brothers/Big Sisters
- Cause-related organizations
  - MADD (Mothers Against Drunk Driving)
  - National Council Against Drug Abuse
  - American Lung Association
  - American Heart Association
  - Audubon Society
- Service organizations
  - Rotary
  - Lions
  - Elks
  - Kiwanis
  - Optimist
  - Soroptimist International
- Human resource managers
- Environmental organizations
  - Sierra Club
  - Audubon Society
- Churches and synagogues
- Real estate developers, brokers, builders, and agents
- Homeowners' associations
- Neighborhood associations
- Welcome wagon

Essential #38: Buy Into a Budget

Your marketing budget is an investment, not an expense. Every agency wishing to improve public perception and marketing results must allocate one or both of their resources: time or money.

When invested wisely, your marketing budget can help you rise above your competition.

Essential Activity #38

Answer the questions about your agency found in Figure 38-1. Highlight those items that need further investigation.

Key Questions	Answers and Comments
Does your agency have a dedicated marketing budget?	
What is your agency's overall marketing budget?	
Does your agency have staff specifically dedicated to marketing, public information, communications, or community outreach?	
Do you have staff with the talent, experience, time, and energy necessary to carry out marketing ideas and strategies?	
Are you able to contract with marketing, public relations, or other professionals who can help carry out marketing activities?	
If no money is currently available in your budget, are you willing and able to find alternative funding sources such as sponsorships and partnerships with other organizations?	
If no money is accessible to finance marketing activities, are you willing to invest time into your program? (You must have money, time, or both to invest in your marketing strategy!)	
Are you willing to change the way you spend your marketing dollars to better promote your camps or agency? (For example, if you spend $50,000 per year to print and mail your program brochure, could you somehow reduce this expense to $40,000 per year and invest $10,000 in new marketing strategies?)	
Does your agency view marketing, advertising, and promotion as expenses or investments?	
Do you have a fundraising organization that might be willing to fund marketing activities?	
Could you contact your local university, community college, or high school marketing clubs to see if an intern (or professor) can assist with your marketing activities for a small stipend or class credit?	

Figure 38-1. Budgeting questions

Essential #39: Money Matters

When it comes to marketing, you have to make an investment to experience results. Unfortunately, no clear-cut formula exists for figuring out how much to spend on your marketing. As a camp or service-based business, you might look to reinvest between 5 and 15 percent of your gross sales into your marketing and business development. Of course, this decision will depend upon many factors.

Before you do anything else you will need to ask yourself, "How much am I willing and able to invest in the marketing of my business?" Unfortunately, no magic formula is available to determine just how much money (or time, for that matter) you must spend to get the desired results. It is important, though, to understand that you have two separate sources of investment capital:

- Your time

- Your money

Again, your marketing should never get in the way of your commitment to quality. But remember, today's marketing will reap tomorrow's customers. Don't be stingy with your time or your dollars. *This process represents your future.* You can budget monthly, quarterly, or yearly, depending upon the complexity and seasonality of your business.

Budget comes in the form of two resources—time and money.

Essential Activity #39

To help you determine your marketing budget, answer the questions in Figure 39-1. You might have to approximate answers rather than procrastinating until you can find a time to calculate precise numbers.

Key Questions	Answers and Comments
What is your gross revenue?	
What is your net profit?	
What products or services do you sell that are the most profitable?	
What products or services do you sell that are the least profitable?	
How many new customers or orders can you efficiently handle without jeopardizing quality?	
How much time are you willing to invest in your marketing efforts?	
How much time are others able to invest in your marketing efforts?	
How long have you been in business?	
How much do your competitors advertise or market?	
The Bottom Line	
What do you feel you can afford in terms of dollars?	
What do you feel you can afford in terms of hours?	

Figure 39-1. The budget bottom line

Essential #40: Invent Time for Marketing

Many successful businesses were built without a penny of advertising. There are literally hundreds of marketing tools and tactics available to you—some of which are very costly and some of which cost absolutely nothing. If you are working with absolutely no marketing budget, have no fear. You still have the precious commodity of time to invest.

Of course, you already work long days. You often work at night and on weekends. When your camps are in full swing, you might be on call 24/7. Therefore, you might be wondering, "Where am I going to find any more time or energy to invest in my marketing activities?" Whether you are an owner, manager, front-line employee, or camp counselor, you are probably spending time on activities that are not totally effective.

Time is a precious resource. Use your time wisely by delegating and eliminating activities that don't serve you and your customers well.

Essential Activity #40

For the next week or so, walk around with a copy of Figure 40-1 in your pocket and jot down everything that comes to your mind.

- In the first part of the figure, jot down every thing and every activity that you love or like about your job, including (but definitely not limited to) the place, the people, the commute, the location, the hours, the customers, the paperwork, the pay, your desk, or even the phone.

- In the second part of the figure, jot down everything you hate or dislike about your job.

- Once you have created this list, start eliminating or delegating the items on the "I hate this about my job" side of the figure (Figure 40-2). Chances are that you are spending too much time and energy on these activities. Activities that people don't enjoy doing are typically activities that they are inefficient at performing. The time engaged in these "hate" tasks could, and should, be spent on marketing and business development.

Think about all tasks, activities, and people involved in your job and your business—duties, staff, hours, geography, location, suppliers, customers, chores, cash flow, accounting. Don't leave out a thing!

I love the following things about my job:	I hate the following things about my job:

For each item on your "hate" list, ask yourself the following questions:

Can this task be eliminated?	
Can this task be changed?	
Is this task absolutely necessary to maintain the quality of my business?	
What would happen if this task didn't get done?	
Is someone else in the company better suited to do this task?	
Could this task be subcontracted to someone else?	
Am I a control freak who is afraid to delegate?	

While the last question is somewhat tongue-in-cheek, it needs to be addressed. Many entrepreneurs and managers have a very difficult time delegating. Chances are, many of the tasks that have landed on your "hate" side could be eliminated, delegated, or changed without hurting the profitability or quality of your camp or organization, while also leaving you the time you need for critical marketing activities.

What activities will I eliminate?	
What activities will I delegate?	
Who will I delegate them to?	
What will I change to save or create more time?	

Figure 40-1. Creating time for marketing

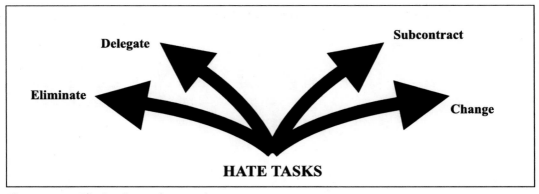

Figure 40-2. Eliminating tasks you detest

Essential #41: Commit to Your Budget

You must make certain commitments to yourself and your marketing. Think of this commitment as a contract with yourself. Sign the contract in Essential Activity #41 to ensure your integrity. In addition, discuss your investment with a mentor, partner, friend, or business associate and have him also sign the contract. This technique is great for ensuring accountability where none typically exists.

Make a commitment to your marketing plan by creating a contract with yourself or others in your organization.

═══ Essential Activity #41 ═══

Put your money and your time where your mouth is. Create a contract with yourself and with a witness to guarantee your commitment to your marketing.

What commitment/investment will you make to reach your marketing goals?

Money: _____ per month/quarter/year

Time: _____ per day/week/month

Signature _____

Coach/Witness _____

Essential #42: Create a Marketing Timeline

Your marketing calendar or timeline is a schedule of when and where your marketing activities will take place. Your calendar tracks your ads, promotions, and publicity on a weekly, monthly, seasonal, and annual basis. It offers a visual picture of how well you are covering your market, and where holes exist in your communication schedule. Your advertising calendar will help you stay consistent. You can track your marketing efforts using a spreadsheet, word processing template, or any other planning tool.

Your timeline is meant to keep you on track and avoid procrastination—not cause unnecessary stress.

Essential Activity #42

Log on to www.microsoft.com and look at the many ready-to-use templates that coordinate with your Microsoft Office programs. Dozens of templates that are specific to marketing are available, including marketing calendars and planning documents.

5

Priced to Sell

"Surely there comes a time when counting the cost and paying the price aren't things to think about any more. All that matters is value—the ultimate value of what one does."
—James Hilton

The price you charge people to attend your camps, rent your facility, buy a sponsorship, or purchase your products is an integral part of your success. The price to attend residential and day camps ranges from thousands of dollars per week to absolutely free. For most people, price is a major consideration when choosing a camp for their child. By applying marketing principals to your pricing strategy, you will attract more prospects and customers to your camps.

Essential #43: Image is Everything

Companies will often deliberately price their product or service at the high end of the spectrum to support an image of exceptional quality. On the other hand, some brands deliberately position themselves as low-price leaders. Figure 43-1 presents examples of brands that use price to stand out from the crowd.

Product	Expensive Brand	Bargain Brand
Car	Jaguar	Kia
Airline	Virgin Atlantic	Southwest
Department Store	Nordstrom	Wal-Mart®
Coffee	Starbucks	7-Eleven®
Pen	Montblanc	Bic®

Figure 43-1. Strategic pricing examples

If you price your camps too low, you may not be able to recover the costs you need to stay in business. Furthermore, a low price tag might cause some potential customers to worry that your quality is inferior. If you are a nonprofit organization, your mission may be to offer low-cost camps for those unable to afford higher-priced options.

If you price your camps too high, you run the risk of excluding customers without affluence. Of course, some consumers equate high prices with high quality. Others are not only willing to pay higher prices, but also seek the prestige associated with luxury items. If you do price your camps higher than your competitors, be prepared to confidently explain what you offer that your competitors don't.

Keep in mind that other costs are involved with attending your camps. These costs include travel, equipment, and intangible costs such as time away from family, friends, work, or school.

Essential Activity #43

Answer the following questions to ensure that you have a solid handle on your camp's image and value. If you're not sure of the answers, ask others in your organization, including your board members. Better yet, contact a few of your customers, who are the true image experts.

- What is the image you want to portray of your camps?

- Do people see you as the Cadillac of camps or do people perceive you as the bargain-basement option?

- What do you offer that your competition does not?

- How much are people willing to pay for the extra value?

Essential #44: Price to Stay in Business

While image is key to pricing your camps, many other variables must be considered to make sure that your pricing structure is a marketing asset. Ultimately, your target customer determines whether your products are priced appropriately. Remember, however, that value is infinitely more important than price in the modern marketplace. Value is truly what customers pay for.

Pricing strategy is dependent upon many criteria, from the economy to your competition.

Essential Activity #44

Each of the factors presented in Figure 44-1 should be considered when evaluating your prices. Consider each aspect and answer the accompanying questions.

	Questions to Consider	Your Response
Profits	More than likely, your camps must generate some type of revenue. Even nonprofit and public agencies typically price camps to recover part or all of their costs. Whether through donations, user fees, sponsorships, or other funding, your camp must pay the bills. No matter how often you doubt it, your customers are aware of the fact that your camp must make a profit to stay in business. Price fairly to yourself, and to your customers. • What does it cost to deliver the camp experience per camper? • What is your total fixed and variable cost to sell one "product"?	
Competition	Don't fall victim to the unknown. Take this opportunity to learn about your competition by referring to or completing your competitive shopping activities. • What do other camps charge? • What do other comparable camps charge?	
Marketplace	Certain parts of the country, for many reasons, have a higher cost of living than others. A loaf of bread in Hawaii is much more expensive than one in Kansas. An apartment in San Francisco can be twice as expensive as the same apartment in nearby Sacramento. Again, take stock of the world around you to ensure fair pricing. • Where does your marketplace fit on the following spectrum?	

Cost of Living
◖---◗
Highest   **Lowest**

The Overall Pricing Questions	
• With all of these factors in mind, are you confident that your product is priced for the greatest marketability? • If not, what will you do to fix it?	

Figure 44-1. Pricing considerations

Essential #45: Let's Make a Deal

Marketers use the term *price consideration* to refer to any pricing strategy, such as a sale or discount, that motivates prospects to take action. Price consideration is often used to stimulate sales in the off-season or motivate new customers to try your product or service. Keep in mind that these considerations must be temporary specials or sales to ensure that customers don't feel manipulated or refuse to pay full price for your products and services later on.

While price promotions can take many innovative forms, always ask yourself the following questions before using discount-pricing techniques:

- Is the offer enough to motivate my customers to action?
- Am I still being profitable?

Go beyond the sale mentality when choosing price promotions. Consider this list of possible price motivators:

- Buy one, get one free
- Buy one, get one half-off
- Family plan for siblings
- Multi-use, multi-session discounts
- Percentage off
- Dollar amount off
- Sale prices

- Early-bird discounts
- Loyalty discounts for repeat campers
- Lifetime membership discounts
- Charter memberships
- Gift certificates
- Coupons

Essential Activity #45

Take a trip to the malls or go online to see how many different types of price promotions you can find. Your head will spin with the number of ways to put a product on sale.

- After exploring what others are doing, choose one or two techniques that would most motivate your target audience without negatively impacting your image.

- How might you use price consideration to encourage new prospects to try your product or service?

Essential #46: Frequent Buyer Programs

Airlines aren't the only ones who can benefit from "frequent-buyer" programs. Frequency programs allow organizations to track, communicate with, and reward their very best customers in countless ways. Your snack shop, concession stand, or gift shop can use frequency programs as well. Reward cards are a simple way for customers to feel appreciated for their loyalty to your agency. As a rule of thumb, consider an approximate "buy 10, get 1 free" ratio. For example:

*   Buy 10 smoothies and get the 11th free

*   Register for nine sessions and get the 10th free

*   Golfers: Buy 10 buckets of balls and get the 11th bucket for free

*   Buy four rounds of golf and get a free bucket of balls

*   Tennis players: Take 10 private lessons and get your racket restrung for free

*   Master swimmers: Swim 10 times and the 11th time is free. Or swim 10 times and get a free pair of swim goggles.

Pizza parlors, airlines, and car rental agencies aren't the only ones who can benefit from a unique punch key tag that rewards customers for loyalty.

Essential Activity #46

Brainstorm a frequent-user program for your camp or programs that might increase sales or participation. How would you track purchases?

Essential #47: Persuade With Premiums

A *premium* is a gift given in exchange for purchase, which can be a great way to motivate people to take action without discounting your price and devaluing your product. The key to choosing a premium is to make sure it is valuable in the eyes of your target audience. Consider offering a camp necessity such as a backpack, water bottle, sleeping bag, laundry bag, or mesh dunk bag. Or offer a premium that your target audience can use immediately, such as music downloads, cell phone accessories, movie tickets, or MP3 players. Shirts, jackets, duffel bags, and caps imprinted with your camp logo can also serve as premiums.

Thousands of premiums like those pictured can be easily imprinted with your camp's name, logo, and tagline. When choosing premiums, be sure to choose items that will motivate your target audience to action.

Essential Activity #47

Look through a magazine or visit a website aimed at your target audience. Notice articles and ads that showcase products coveted by your customers.

*   Make a list of premium ideas that you might use to encourage participation or registration.

*   Make a list of possible sponsors or donors who might be willing to donate items for use as premiums in exchange for promotional consideration in camp brochures or literature.

Essential #48: Bundle Products With Marketing Partners

When people sign up for camp, they are often given a long list of items and equipment they need to bring. Residential campers, especially, must buy or borrow everything from sleeping bags to backpacks. By working with local sporting goods stores or other retailers, you might be able to bundle products with registration fees to create a super-convenient, one-price package that includes registration fees and all the camping equipment the first-time camper needs.

Another way to capitalize on a camp–retail partnership is to find businesses willing to offer deep discounts to your customers who need to purchase gear and equipment. These types of marketing partnerships greatly benefit everyone, including your customers. For example, when campers receive their equipment list, you might also attach a $25 gift certificate from the sporting goods store to be used on their purchase of $100 or more. In exchange for distributing the coupons to your campers, you might ask the retailer to put information about your camps in their employee break room, in customer shopping bags, or at their counter.

Package products with your partners. After signing up for camp, what gear do campers buy? Why not create a limited registration package that includes equipment? It's a convenient and creative pricing option.

Essential Activity #48

Contact your chamber of commerce or use your local phone directory to make a list of potential marketing partners.

- Refer to your equipment list and ask yourself, "Who sells the items on this list?"

- Contact at least five businesses on your list.

- Ask them if they would like you to refer your campers to their store when looking to buy equipment for camp. Of course they would!

- To make the referral process easier, ask them to provide you with discount coupons or gift certificates that you can attach directly to the equipment list.

Essential #49: Sell Gift Certificates

Help parents, aunts, uncles, grandparents, and other relatives and friends give the gift of camping to your repeat campers. Offer gift certificates to parents via email and suggest that they forward the idea along to others. You can also give gift certificates as a form of price promotion. For example, track camper birthdays and surprise them with a card and a $10 dollar gift certificate from your camp's director. Or send a holiday card complete with a "gift card" that can be used toward any camp tuition.

Gift Certificate

Parents, grandparents, aunts, and uncles will especially love the idea of giving the gift of camp.

Essential Activity #49

Create a gift certificate campaign that ties in with a holiday or seasonal event. Thanksgiving, Christmas, Hanukkah, New Year's Day, and Valentine's Day are well timed to promote early-bird camp registration.

Essential #50: Give Groups a Break

The travel and tourism industry commonly offers group discounts to stimulate sales and increase volume. For example, if you pull together a group of friends, co-workers, neighbors, or relatives who take the same cruise, you can negotiate a reduced rate or earn a free cabin. If you book 10 rooms at a resort for your family reunion, you may get a 25 percent discount off the entire block of rooms—and free breakfast, too!

While many camps rent facilities to groups, you can expand this concept to other products. Why not use this same pricing and marketing strategy to promote camp registration? Group pricing makes great sense. Rather than selling one camp registration at a time, group sales enable you to sell to one "leader" who acts as your word-of-mouth sales agent. In some cases, you may already have groups, troops, or teams in place. In other cases, you may have to work with customers to uncover or create groups. Adult groups are prime candidates for this type of marketing, especially if you are looking for off-season business. The following ideas can get you started:

*   Birthday parties and celebrations
    (not just for kids)
*   Extended families
*   Game groups (bunko, bingo, poker)
*   Play groups
*   Business groups
*   Neighborhood associations
*   Service clubs (Rotary, Lions, Kiwanis, Soroptimist, Optimist)
*   Sports teams
*   Churches, synagogues, temples, etc.
*   Support groups (medical, emotional, recovery)

Give volume discounts for reunions, clubs, and other large groups.

Essential Activity #50

Contact a local travel agency or the group sales department of a hotel, airline, or cruise line.

- What is their definition of a group?

- Find out what types of group discounts, incentives, and premiums they offer.

- Make a list of at least five ideas that could be applied to your camps. Go beyond discounts and include gifts, incentives, or transportation.

Find out what types of groups are currently customers of your camps.

- If you already have a group pricing program, enhance and promote it to other groups.

- If you don't have a group pricing program, create one.

- Make a list of other groups in your community that might use your camp facilities or bring multiple campers to your programs.

- Draft and send a letter to group leaders announcing your enhanced group discount program.

6

Motivating Messages

"When dealing with people, let us remember we are not dealing with creatures of logic. We are dealing with creatures of emotion, creatures bustling with prejudices and motivated by pride and vanity."
—Dale Carnegie

The goal of marketing is to motivate your target customer to some kind of action. As you strengthen your marketing foundation, gain new perspective, and commit your plan to writing, you must figure out how you will reach and motivate your customers. Armed with new insight, enthusiasm, and information, you are ready to create your marketing message. While you have literally millions of things you can say, do, and show to communicate to your target audience, some essential tactics will help you stand apart from the crowd and get your message noticed.

Essential #51: Don't Be all Talk, no Action

While good will and awareness are important, marketing should demand (or at least request or stimulate) some kind of action on the part of the recipient. Ultimately, you want your prospect to register for camp, send you a donation, volunteer his time, or apply for a job. Remember, camp is a big decision. Your prospect may have to take some baby steps before he becomes your customer.

Talk is cheap when it comes to marketing. It's time to put your ideas into place and take action.

The first thing to ask before designing a marketing tool—whether it is a brochure or a website—is, "What do I want the person to *do* after seeing, reading, hearing, receiving, or passing by *this* marketing message?" Consider these possible answers:

- Log on to your website

- Send an email

- Register for a camp, class, program, or event

- Come to an information event—an open house, orientation, or other event where prospects can learn more

- Fill out a form—job and scholarship applications and medical and photo release forms may be a necessary part of your customer and staff process

- Call to schedule an appointment—probably the most common objective in business-to-business marketing

- Give a lead or referral—common when marketing to gatekeepers, or current or past customers

- Welcome your call—used to turn a cold call into a warm, or even hot, prospect

- Come in for a visit—the most common marketing tool if you have a showroom, store, or facility where the customer comes to you

- Book a meeting, event, retreat or convention—very common for those who rent facilities for parties, special events, weddings, meetings, sporting events, etc.

- Schedule a familiarization trip or site inspection—this concept was coined by the travel industry, but could be used by camps whose rentals depend upon clients becoming more familiar with the set-up, facilities, amenities, space, equipment, location, products, people, etc.

- Request more information—why send out a costly marketing kit, video, or promotion to someone who will never have a need for your product? Your initial marketing piece might be a pre-qualifier to a more complete (and more expensive) packet.

- Fill out a questionnaire—knowledge is power! Do you want to gather research, data, feedback, or ideas? You may need to build a database for future marketing programs.

- Place an order—In some instances, the goal of your marketing vehicle will be to get the recipient to place an order. If, for example, you sell logo apparel, camping equipment, or other gear, create a promotion that gets your customer to make a purchase via mail, phone, fax, or email.

Essential Activity #51

Your next marketing tool must be planned.

- What *specific action* do you want your customer to take after receiving your marketing message?

- Review the options presented in Essential #51 and add your own. Are you trying to close the deal or just get your foot in the door?

- What actions will your prospects take after they have seen (or heard) your marketing message?

Essential #52: Imagine Their Day

What's a day in the life of your customer like? Does he toss and turn all night, only to be jarred awake by the alarm clock? Does he go off to school or work after gobbling a bowl of sugary cereal? Or does he prefer a hot breakfast complete with all the fixings? Does he drive in a car, take a bus, or ride the subway? Does he walk? After work or school, what does he do? Watch TV? Play on the computer? Go to tutoring or participate in sports, music, or arts activities? Does your customer have to answer email or the phone? Does he need to finish homework or pay bills?

Although it would be nice to think that your customer is sitting around just waiting for your marketing message to come his way, the truth is this person is probably very busy—just like you. Your customer's brain is already filled with millions of pieces of information. Every day he is bombarded with hundreds, even thousands, of advertising and marketing offers.

The key to breaking through that clutter of information depends upon how well you know your target audience. You must compete like a champion for your customer's attention to keep your marketing out of the literal and metaphorical landfill.

Essential Activity #52

You have already explored what makes your customer tick. To break through customer clutter, you must put yourself further into his shoes, empathize with him, and feel what his days are like. Highlight the tasks below that could "clutter" your customer's attention. Add your own to the list and talk to him to get the whole cluttered story.

- Wears many hats
- Juggles many projects
- Has mail to open, sort, and read
- Has homework to finish
- Returns emails
- Visits websites
- Has social events to attend
- Attends recreation activities

- Makes and returns phone calls
- Attends meetings and appointments
- Sits in traffic or carpools
- Copes with interruptions
- Has decisions to make
- _____
- _____

Essential #53: Be at the Right Place at the Right Time

When it comes to competing for your customer's attention, timing is a critical factor. Consider the following three ways to time and word your promotion so that it is noticed and eventually acted upon.

Have it arrive at the moment he is ready to buy—Reaching the customer at the very moment that he is ready to buy is every marketer's fantasy! Unfortunately, it is also very difficult to control. After all, what are the chances that your customer is going to need your product or service or be looking for a camp at the exact instant when he gets your brochure in the mail, reads your article in the newspaper, hears your ad on the radio, or sees it in the newspaper or in his mailbox?

Of course, you can market to this "ready to buy" audience through point-of-purchase advertising. In addition, gatekeepers can greatly help. Your partners, who are already in tune with your target audience, can alert you when a contact is ripe for what you have to sell. For example, if you have developed a relationship with a friendly competitor, they may refer a customer to your camps during a session when their camps are full. You can offer to do the same for them.

Word your promotion so that he will remember you when it's time to buy—Frequency is very important. Create a marketing message or promotion that is frequent, memorable, or permanent. Doing so makes perfect timing less important. When your customer needs your product or service, he will think of you.

Word your promotion in such a way that you motivate him to act or buy "now"—Can you offer your prospect something so valuable that he would be crazy not to act immediately? Everyone loves a great deal, to feel like they got something for nothing. Do you have a once-in-a-lifetime (or even once-a-year) opportunity?

Timing is everything. Get in sync with your target audience's schedule.

This computer mouse pad is a permanent and useful reminder of Dayton, Ohio's parks and recreation department.

Essential Activity #53

- What kind of promotional tool could you develop that your customer would want to keep that could also be imprinted with your name, website, or registration dates?

- What type of promotional item would keep your name in front of your target audience for weeks, months, or even years?

- If possible, look around your target audience's room, desk, home, office, or classroom. What types of promotional items are already in use?

- Have you considered a mouse pad, calendar, magnet, T-shirt, backpack, water bottle, lunch bag, pen, pencil, or ruler?

- What types of functional items might be imprinted for your gatekeepers to remind them that you want their referrals?

- Log onto www.advisorsmarketing.com to see thousands of promotional product ideas.

Essential #54: Solve Their Problems

Now that you've explored your customer's needs and concerns, it is time to communicate that "We are your solution! The most essential marketing messages are solution based. Don't assume that your customers know that they have or could have the problem you solve. Remind them that the problem might occur later (e.g., summer boredom), even if it's not an issue in March, when registration begins.

Your customers have problems, aches, and pains. Let them know that you can make the hurt go away and offer First Aid for Summer Boredom.

Essential Activity #54

What problems do you solve for your target customer better than anyone else?

- Refer back to your customer interview forms for more insight (Essential Activity #17).

- Go online to do a quick search for new research pertaining to issues facing your target audience (e.g., social issues facing youth, family crises, Baby Boomer concerns).

Essential #55: Stress Benefits

As you develop your marketing materials, it's easy to confuse benefits with features, but it is important to know the difference, especially when writing and speaking about your camp and its products. As you write program descriptions, flyers, advertising copy, and other marketing tools, take care not to slip into "features-only language." Review these simple definitions:

- A feature is what the product or service *is*—who, what, when, where, and how much.

- A benefit is what the product or service does for customers or the community— why they participate, why it is so important, how it impacts their lives, and what they get out of the program.

Essential Activity #55

Review the following example, which covers an urban youth camp. Then, create a detailed list of benefits that your product delivers in each of the four benefit categories.

Program Name: Urban Camping for High-Risk Youth

List the types of people or groups who use the "product":

Direct participants/users:
- Teens from low-income families
- First-time juvenile (misdemeanor) offenders
- Foster children

Indirect participants/users:
- Parents/guardians of teens

Gatekeepers:
- Teachers
- Social workers
- School counselors
- Juvenile justice system
- Churches

Next, list benefit outcomes of the program in terms of the four benefit areas:

Individual/personal:

■ Teen participants

- Discover ways to resolve conflict and work through anger
- Experience elevated self-esteem
- Learn job skills
- Gain respect for self and others
- Experience teamwork
- Learn to trust adult role models
- Diverts teens from negative, destructive activities
- Learn how to access community resources
- Meet new friends
- Create new memories

■ Parents

- Don't have to worry about children's safety and security
- Don't have to pay for this free program
- Transportation is safe and provided

Community/social:

- May reduce juvenile crime
- Helps create productive citizens
- Encourages neighborhood pride

Economic:

- Future tax-paying citizens are developed
- Volunteer activities offset staff costs
- Program is self-sustaining through sponsorship dollars

Environmental:

- Teaches respect for the environment
- Teens participate in park clean-up activities that beautify parkland

Essential #56: Answer Questions

When it comes to website traffic, the FAQ (frequently asked questions) section is one of the most popular. Your customers have questions and you have answers. Sometimes your customers have questions specifically related to camp, but they also have lots of questions related to the benefits of camp. For example:

- Your camp has a strict no-bullying policy. Can you answer questions in your marketing materials that provide information about why kids bully, what to do if you are being bullied, how to get help if you are a bully, etc.? You may hook prospects with the bullying information. Once they are engaged, you can sell them on your amazing camp that never tolerates bullying!

- Perhaps your camp has developed a new, healthier menu. Could you attract new customers to your camp by offering answers to childhood nutrition and fitness questions? In other words, your prospect might be looking for solutions to get their picky eater to kick the sugar habit. They may not be looking for camp information. But, if you hook them with the answers to the questions they seek, they will also see that you offer solutions beyond the good nutrition information.

What questions do your customers have about camps and camping? Answer them and you bring customers one step closer to registration.

Essential Activity #56

Your customers and prospects have many questions that pertain to your camp's mission and purpose. You and your staff are a wealth of information.

- What questions do your customers have about camp?

- What question do your customers have about life?

- How do you provide answers?

Essential #57: Captivate With Copy

Make your marketing unforgettable by developing a distinct theme that can create continuity throughout your campaign. Make people smile, think, or reminisce about their past. Use curiosity or shock value to get customers to sit up and take notice of what you have to say. Don't offend, but don't be afraid to do something out of the ordinary, especially if it gets people to laugh and remember. Use language to relay your competitive edge.

Stop your prospect in his tracks with copy that asks a question, challenges him, or entices him to hear or read more. Great promotional copy brings your message to life by telling a compelling story, inspiring the imagination, turning on emotions, or making the reader laugh. Even the most ordinary program and facility descriptions must radiate with visual adjectives and modifiers. Shed light on your solutions (*lose* weight, *eliminate* stress, *decrease* loneliness) or showcase enhancements (*gain* self-confidence, *acquire* career skills, *increase* stamina).

Essential Activity #57

Use the following list of marketing power words to transform passive written and verbal communication into action-oriented copy.

Words that express an enhancement to something positive:

• Accomplish	• Feel	• Learn	• Refresh
• Achieve	• Find	• Maintain	• Restore
• Acquire	• Gain	• Make	• Retain
• Add	• Get	• Master	• Refurbish
• Advance	• Grow	• Polish	• Renew
• Attain	• Heighten	• Procure	• Return
• Better	• Help	• Profit	• Shrink
• Create	• Identify	• Progress	• Stomp out
• Discover	• Imagine	• Promote	• Top
• Enhance	• Improve	• Reach	• Uncover
• Exceed	• Increase	• Rediscover	• Win
• Explore	• Jump start	• Refine	

Words that express a solution to a problem:

- Amend
- Break free
- Correct
- Cure
- Decrease

- Diminish
- Eliminate
- Fix
- Get rid of
- Help

- Lessen
- Lose
- Lower
- Overtake
- Overcome

- Reduce
- Shrink
- Stomp out
- Transcend

Transition words and phrases:

- Because
- In order to

- So that
- Then

- To
- While

- Because

Essential #58: Grab With Graphics

A picture is still worth a thousand words! Grab the reader with dynamic graphics. From an unusual illustration to a fantastic photograph, go beyond the ordinary camp graphics to cause people to stop in their tracks. Tie graphics into an overall campaign theme or your global benefits message.

Use strong images in your marketing materials and adhere to design principles that work for your target audience. If you're marketing to seniors, for example, remember that type should be 12 points or larger. With a few exceptions, most young children can't read beyond their grade level—and preschool children can't read at all!

Learn to love white space. Remember that your introductory marketing piece needs to capture attention rather than give all the details. Once they're hooked, subsequent pieces can offer more facts and particulars.

Photos and graphics should grab attention. Merge a unique photo with great copy for a message they'll flip over.

Essential Activity #58

Log on to one of the many stock photo sites, such as photos.com, freeimages.com, istockphotos.com, and jupiterimages.com. These databases have tens of millions of very high-quality photographs and illustrations sure to give your promotion the impact it needs to break through the clutter.

Essential #59: Color Their World

Color is one of the most powerful of all design forces. By understanding how your customers interpret color, you can harness its strength to create more motivating marketing.

Color can stop people in their tracks—literally. It can draw attention, lead the eye, and add emphasis. It can be used to show continuation and relatedness, or it can differentiate. Color generates emotions, connections, and associations.

If you are marketing to an international audience, you will want to check with your target to ensure that your choice of color is not offensive or sending the wrong signals. For example, yellow in the United States is a great attention grabber and signifies warmth, happiness, and sunshine. In France, however, yellow means jealousy. The Chinese view yellow as a sacred color and the Greeks associate yellow with sadness.

While different cultures may interpret colors differently, the explanations that follow are American-based:

- Red means excitement in advertising design. It is commonly used for automobile and food advertising. Red is equated with passion, sex, danger, velocity, and power.

- Yellow is a great attention grabber in advertising design. It means sunshine, warmth, and happiness. It is the first color the human eye processes.

- Blue represents reliability, trust, security, and technology, which is why businesses often use blue, green, teal, or gray in their advertising. Blue also represents coolness and belonging.

- Black represents sophistication and strength. It is elegant and seductive. For the right product, black is a great color.

- Green is a cool, fresh color. It represents nature and spring.

- Purple means royalty. It is dignified and refined.

- Pink is soft and feminine. It conveys security and sweetness.

- White stands for cleanliness and purity in advertising design. It is youthful, but it is not necessarily for young people. Young people (teens and "tweens") prefer more trendy colors, like mauve and teal. You must also consider white space when designing advertising design. Without white space, you can't read the text. Photos lose their impact and the ad loses balance. White space may be the most important component of your advertising design.

- Gold means expensive and high-class.

- Orange is playful. It brings to mind autumn leaves, warmth, and vibrancy.

- Silver is prestigious. It represents coldness and science.

Don't forget that every season has its own colors and fashion changes. If you are trying to be trendy with your advertising design, then you have to keep up with the trends.

The right color can create a sense of security, warmth, joy, or calm.

Essential Activity #59

- Using your computer's word processing or art program, type your name or your camp name in a very large font (100+ points).

- Start by viewing your "art" in black.

- Then recolor your name using the colors listed in Essential #59.

- What is your emotional reaction as your camp name goes through its colorful makeover?

- Does your camp logo have a color scheme that is consistent?

- Could or should your logo's color scheme be updated?

- Why or why not?

Essential #60: Emphasize Exclusivity

"People will buy anything that is 'one to a customer.'"
—Sinclair Lewis

Waiting lists are a reality for many camps. You may be bound by space, staff, equipment, and other factors that force you to limit registration or enrollment. No one wants to be turned away when trying to register for camp. No parent wants to disappoint their child. No child wants to be left behind as their friends drive off for a summer of fun. And no sponsor wants to be told that they can't attach their name to your highly publicized event because their competitor has beaten them to the punch.

Limited availability, quantity, time, and space are great motivators to inspire a quick response. Don't bluff or mislead your customers with false limitations, but if your offer is truly limited and very attractive, then tell your customers. They won't want to miss out.

Essential Activity #60

Many of your camps and programs are available in a limited supply to a limited number of campers or customers. Consider the following questions:

- How can you highlight these limits in your marketing message in a way that motivates action?

- What special offers could you create that might be available only for a limited time or a limited number of customers?

- What else could you offer that is limited in time, quantity, space, etc.?

Essential #61: Make Them Winners

Contests, games, and sweepstakes are great ways to get people interested and engaged in your marketing message. While your customers may not be ready to register for camp, they may be motivated by the chance to win or compete for a prize.

Camp customers, especially, love interaction and competition. Prizes don't always have to be expensive to be effective. Often, prospects will be motivated by small prizes or rewards that cost nothing at all. For example, offer winners a VIP parking spot or the chance to have their picture on the cover of your brochure.

One of the other reasons that contests are so effective is that they offer great publicity opportunities. The media love covering stories about contests that are wacky, weird, and uncommon. Television and newspapers look for visual stories such as the world's largest, biggest, longest, or tallest anything. How high is the world's highest s'more? How many hot dogs do your campers eat over the course of a summer? If all of those hot dogs were stacked end to end, how high would they be?

If you exhibit at trade shows, expos, or community fairs, use contests to attract attention to your booth. Guess how many? Fill out a form to win. When people fill out their forms, make sure to capture valuable data for future marketing activities.

Everyone loves a winner and everyone loves a chance to win something. Prizes can be tangible or intangible.

Essential Activity #61

Brainstorm a list of contests, sweepstakes, or games that might stimulate action and generate a little publicity at the same time. Keep your target audience in mind as you develop your list.

- Where will the contest take place?

- What should you give away?

- How big does the prize need to be?

- Can you partner with another business that might supply the prize in exchange for promotional consideration?

Essential #62: Invite Prospects to a Special Event

As a camp, you are in the event business! Your camps are events. Every talent show, family fun day, and celebration is an event of varying complexity. Because you already have extensive experience creating and executing events, you can easily apply these skills to developing a promotional event, too.

To be effective, your marketing events must attract your target audience or gatekeepers to learn more about what you offer. Effective events can happen at your facilities or off-site. You can host events alone or in partnership with other organizations. No matter what type of event you choose, make sure you promote your camps, message, and brand in as many places as possible.

Special events don't need to be huge extravaganzas. They just need to be special in the eyes of your target audiences. Consider the following options:

• Concert	• Open house	• Alumni reunion
• Festival	• Networking event	• Book signing
• Movie	• Designer showcase	• Flea market/gear swap
• Tournament	• Fashion show	• Product demonstration
• Sports clinic	• Party	• Celebrity appearance
• Seminar	• User club	

Many special events are celebratory and joyful. Music, art, and performances create an exciting, high-energy atmosphere. Take advantage of this collective good mood to spread your positive message. Your goal is to get attendees to associate your organization or camp with the quality of the event. Try to incorporate your logo and message in all event collateral, promotional tools, and signage, including the following:

• Programs	• Promotional product giveaways	• Follow-up and thank-you letters
• Banners		
• Signage	• Audio introductions and remarks from the stage	• Tickets
• T-shirts		• Awards and certificates
	• All press materials	

Everyone loves receiving an invitation in the mail. Create an event—complete with decorations—to generate off-season communication with past campers, alumni, and prospects.

Essential Activity #62

Celebrities are a great way to build traffic, enthusiasm, and publicity for any event. But it doesn't take a Hollywood starlet, rock star, or sports hero to attract customers. A celebrity only needs to be a celebrity in the eyes of your target audience.

Review the following list and then make a list of celebrities that will appeal to your target audience.

- Musician
- Speaker
- Author
- Politician
- Sports hero
- Movie or TV star

- Former movie or TV personality
- Children's character
- Business leader
- Magician
- Street performer (juggler, mime, etc.)

Essential #63: Free Anything!

"Free" is the most powerful word in marketing. What can you give away that will motivate your customers while still maintaining your profit margin? This giveaway could even be an added-value service—something special your competitors don't offer or that will delight and surprise your customers. Consider the following possibilities:

- Gifts—Gifts don't have to be expensive, just useful for your audience.

- Equipment—Campers need so much gear.

- Consultation—Does your time have value?

- Information—Provide special reports, articles, and surveys.

- Samples—Don't let shampoo companies have all the fun. Samples allow people to try before they buy. Offer a free mini-camp to let prospects experience the fun without having to make the costly investment.

- Merchandise—Buy one item, get something else for free.

- Gift certificate—Be creative. Could you and a partner trade gift certificates?

- Instruction—Do you sell a product or service that needs explanation to be used efficiently?

- Seminar—What type of workshop or seminar would your target customer come to? What do they need to learn?

- Baby-sitting service—If your customers have kids, but need to come to your offices to register, attend orientation, or use your services, then make it easy for them to do business with you by entertaining their "little distractions."

- Installation—Can you install or set up your product for your customers to ensure that everything is working properly?

- Transportation—Can you give campers a free lift to camp or make transporting campers more convenient for parents?

Essential Activity #63

Make a list of things you could you offer for free to your customers to motivate them to action.

7

Choose Your Vehicles

"When one door closes another door opens; but we so often look so long and so regretfully upon the closed door that we do not see the ones which open for us."
—Alexander Graham Bell

Once you have determined what you are going to say, it's time to decide where you are going to say it. Your marketing plan is not complete until you select the very best media to *carry* your marketing message. Marketing "vehicles" literally *drive* or *move* the message to your target audience.

Marketing vehicles range from very high-tech to very intimate and high-touch. Some are totally free and some cost millions of dollars—a 30-second television spot on the Super Bowl costs more than two million dollars! But, just because you spend a lot of money doesn't guarantee that your media will work. As you consider the ever-expanding list of media options that follow, always remember that even the most powerful (or expensive) vehicle in the universe will be totally ineffective if it doesn't reach your target audience or if the message doesn't motivate.

Media can be segmented into four categories, each of which is explored in this chapter.

- Personal selling and face-to-face marketing
- Promotions
- Mass media advertising
- Publicity and public relations

Some media tools can fall into more than one category. For example, the Internet can be a very intimate, personal selling tool, and it can also be used to build public relations. Newspapers, magazines, television, and radio can be used for advertising and for publicity. Contests fall under the "promotions" category, but can be advertised using the mass media. As you'll discover, the categories are not as important as choosing a mix of communication tools that will reach and attract your target audience with a meaningful and motivating message.

Essential #64: Don't Bite Off More Than You Can Chew

Marketing is a balancing act. Be careful not to attract more customers or campers than you can accommodate. The key to blending the perfect marketing mix is to choose vehicles within your time and dollar budget that work best to reach your chosen target audience.

After considering your promotional vehicle options, you must decide on the ones that will best work for you. The more you have zeroed in on a specific target audience, the easier it is to find effective media. Your media mix will depend upon the following elements:

- Your target audience
- Your monetary budget
- Your time budget
- The availability of stock or manpower—Be careful not to attract more customers than you and your team can feasibly handle. Would your customers appreciate standing in line or being put on eternal hold?

When it comes to your marketing objectives, don't bite off more than you can chew.

Essential Activity #64

Before choosing your vehicles, clarify how much business you can handle. Imagine that you are over-the-top successful with your marketing efforts and have attracted way too many people to your activities, events or camps.

- In your case, how many is too many?

- What systems do you have in place when camps or programs get "full"?

- Are waiting lists a sign of marketing success or a marketing failure?

- What are the negative implications of waiting lists and "turning people away" when programs are at capacity?

- What could be the long-term implications of turning people away?

- What could you do to avoid disappointment or negative public relations that occur when "demand exceeds supply"?

- Where does your target audience get its information (radio, TV, specific newspapers, friends, business associates, etc.)?

- Where does your target audience "hang out"? Where do they go for entertainment and to socialize?

- What type of radio stations and television shows do they watch?

- How do they make buying decisions about your particular product or service?

Essential #65: Go to the Source

A group of people is available that can tell you exactly which media to choose. This group has almost all the answers you seek to make sure that you don't waste your money on media that will never be seen, heard, or read by those you need to reach to meet your goals. Who are they?

Your customers, of course! Even if you are looking to reach new types of people, your current customers have insight into reaching diverse audiences, too. No one knows what kids want more that kids. While parents can offer guidance, they don't have all the answers. Engage your campers in your media-selection process and you will maximize your investment.

Choosing marketing vehicles is not a secret. Your customers have the answers you need.

Essential Activity #65

Once again, write down your answers to the following questions (or refer back to your customer interviews from Essential Activity #17):

- Where does your target audience get its information (radio, TV, specific newspapers, friends, business associates, etc.)?

- Where does your target audience "hang out"? Where do they go for entertainment and to socialize?

- What type of radio stations and television shows do they watch?

- How do they make buying decisions about your particular product or service?

Essential #66: Think in Steps

Your experience as both a consumer and marketer tells you that most people don't make impulsive decisions about things as important as where to send their child to camp. It will likely take repeated exposures to your message for your prospects to take action. The more exposures they have, the more likely they are to recall your message. The more vehicles you use, the more likely it becomes that you will reach more prospects.

How many times your prospect needs to hear, see, or be exposed to your message before taking action depends upon the following:

- The complexity of your product or service
- Your target audience's general awareness and understanding of your industry
- Your target audience's existing awareness of your company or organization
- The cost of your product or service (the more costly and complex, the more steps typically required)

Some people will come into the marketing process ready, willing, and able to buy your product or service. Your product may not be very complicated, or your prospect might be a repeat customer or be well aware of you camp's quality. Sometimes, however, you will need to be educate, woo, motivate, and nurture your prospect through the entire process.

The following marketing steps parallel your customer's "steps to the buy." Choose media that will reach prospects where they are in terms of their buying process—from totally unaware to ready to sign on the dotted line!

Step 1: Create awareness—Is your prospect *unaware* of his need for your product or service? If so, you may need to promote the overall benefits of camp—any camp—to your prospects.

Step 2: Introduce—Is your prospect *unfamiliar* with your product, service, or company? In other words, your prospect believes in the benefits of camp, but doesn't know that your camp exists.

Step 3: Get your foot in the door—Do you need to get in front of your client to discuss ideas, details, or needs before a sale can be made?

Step 4: Educate and gain trust—Does your prospect need to learn how your product can make his life better? Does he need to develop trust for you, your staff, or your organization.

Step 5: Finalize the sale—Do you want to finalize the sale? Of course you do! Give prospects as reason to act now.

Step 6: Follow-up post-sale—Is it necessary for you to keep in communication with your customer after the initial sale? Of course it is!

Choosing a camp is not an impulsive decision. Lead prospects through that phase of the buying process.

Essential Activity #66

In terms of your target audience, determine which steps are required to reach your marketing objectives. As you consider your marketing vehicles, choose at least one tactic for each of the six steps to walk a prospect from awareness to repeat customer.

Essential #67: Inventory Your Media—Options, Options Everywhere

When it comes to choosing media, unless you are a brand-new organization or camp, your media mix is not a blank canvas. Whether you inherited certain media tools or chose them yourself, some vehicles are already in your marketing toolkit.

A media inventory is a complete list of all of your existing and upcoming marketing tools. Your inventory might also explore promotional strategies used in the past. After all, something that didn't work in the past might work in the present.

Look around your camp, office, desk, date book, and computer. Look at the many communication and marketing tools you already use. Everywhere you see your logo, you see a marketing tool. From the most basic business cards and letterhead to more involved websites and promotional tools, you have a long list of media at your fingertips.

In addition, you and your staff comprise a busy sales and customer service team delivering messages to individual and group audiences each and every day. As you look at your calendar, you already know that brochures and registration packets will be printed and mailed to past and future campers. Even your emails and outgoing voicemail message are marketing vehicles. While your current list of marketing tools may have been carefully selected and scheduled, it's more likely that your media mix is a combination of long-time standards and hit-or-miss vehicles.

You already use many methods to spread the word about your camps and programs.

Essential Activity #67

Make a list of all of the ways your customer could possibly learn about your products. You might have to talk to others in your organization to find out what they have planned as well.

This list should not feature what you'd like to do, but instead include actual, upcoming opportunities (Figure 67-1). Don't forget to list your "on-site" marketing opportunities (registration, games, rehearsals, nutrition fair). Of course, no list would be complete without word-of-mouth.

- Begin with all of the big activities and tools (e.g., brochure, website).

- List all of your upcoming ads in print and broadcast media.

- Then add in all of your high-traffic events (summer concerts, festivals, tournaments, fairs, etc.).

- Add in all of your lower-traffic events (classes, dances, expos, clubs, leagues, etc.).

- Continue with outdoor marketing (banners, marquee, signage, billboards, etc.)

- Use the lists included in Essentials #70 through 74 to spark other upcoming opportunities.

Opportunities	Examples
The Basics	Brochure, website
Mass Media Advertising	
Big Events	
Smaller Events	
Publicity News Releases Presentations	
Promotion	
On-site	
Outdoor and Transit	
Word-of-Mouth	

Figure 67-1. Media inventory

Essential #68: Come Together

Whether you are part of a multifaceted organization such as a park and recreation department or a stand-alone camp, your customers might take many paths to learn about your programs and how they fill their needs. Remember that new prospects, especially, may not know that they want what you have. They may be looking for a stress-free Thanksgiving, but don't know about your Thanksgiving Family Camp. Parents may be looking for summer child care, but not know that you offer an extended-day camp that meets all of their summer child care needs—and more!

Teen boys might be looking to meet girls and find a fun job, but have no idea that your camp is the perfect fit. Teens shouldn't have to (and probably won't) look at four or five different sections of your brochure or website to learn which of your agency's products are targeted and available to them.

Teens, like everyone else, want to see all of their options in one convenient place—extreme sports, traditional sports, fitness, cultural arts, volunteer opportunities, dances, trips, counselor-in-training (CIT) programs, junior lifeguard training, job opportunities, college prep clubs, etc. Ultimately, your goal should be to create a marketing campaign just for teens incorporating all of the products targeted to teens. By creating a global inventory with others in your organization, you can blend budgets, maximize results, and take advantage of each other's activities.

For example, the teen center has a dance in November, while CIT orientation begins in January. Cross-promote the CIT training at the dance to reach new CITs.

Get together with other departments and noncompeting organizations to compile a complete list of upcoming media opportunities.

Essential Activity #68

Take your media inventory to the next level by hosting a get-together with others in your agency, neighboring agencies, or the community to create a collective media inventory. While this activity is best done in a face-to-face brainstorming session with representatives from each organization or department, you can begin by creating an online version of your communal inventory.

Once together, you can brainstorm ways to merge your media to increase your reach and effectiveness. Imagine the sophisticated tactics you might be able to afford if you were to pool resources. At the very least, discuss ways to refer customers to one another.

Create your invite list by answering the following questions. Update your inventory on a regular basis—at least quarterly—to let your partners in on new opportunities.

- Who else in your organization or community is already in touch with your target audience?

- Who else offers camps to your target audience at a totally different price point?

- Who else in your community is already in touch with your target audience?

- Who offers camps or programs similar to, but not exactly like, yours?

- If applicable, who communicates with your customers in your "off-season"?

Essential #69: Eliminate the Marketing Maze

Many agencies regularly publish a detailed brochure, activity guide, or catalog of classes to promote all of their products in one complete resource. Your website might also list all of your offerings under one domain name. While it may be convenient for your agency to have one big marketing tool, it's important to remember that it may not be the best way to reach your customers.

When searching for a camp or other activity, most people are only concerned with products that "fit" their needs. No one wants to work to navigate their way through a complex organizational chart to find what they need. As you know, people have problems and want to be rescued by solutions.

For example, teens want to find everything for them without having to sift through programs for babies and older adults. Parents of toddlers don't want to sort through pages and pages of camps and activities for older kids only to find the programs for toddlers buried in the back of your brochure.

Marketing material should not confuse, but rather guide prospects through the buying process.

Essential Activity #69

Evaluate your marketing tools from a customer's point of view.

- How target-audience-friendly are your marketing vehicles?

- What can you do to help your target audience escape from the marketing maze and make their way directly to your message?

- What might it take for you to create marketing tools that are specific to your unique target audiences?

Essential #70: Make Intimate Connections With Marketing "Laser Beams"

Some marketing methods are delivered one message at a time. Many of these messages are sales activities. Because of their extreme accuracy, these messages are called marketing "laser beams." These techniques are part of almost every business' marketing program in one form or another.

Characteristics of laser beams:

- Pinpoint accuracy
- Little or no dollar investment
- High time investment
- Possible immediate response
- Two-way communication

Laser beams are best for:

- Building relationships with end users and gatekeepers
- Qualifying prospects
- Gathering information
- Those with no money, but lots of time
- Finalizing details
- Inexpensive ongoing communication
- Those willing to invest in some training to perfect skills

Examples of marketing laser beams:

- Canvassing and cold calls
- Sales calls
- Email marketing
- Physical visits to the customer's home or business
- Telemarketing
- Personal letters and notes
- Collateral packages (brochures, business cards, invoices, etc.)
- Networking

- Specialty advertising, gifts, and promotional items delivered via:
  - Personal visits
  - Mail to individuals
  - Customer picks-up
  - Part of a package
  - Interior point-of-purchase signage and displays
  - Exterior storefront signage

Face-to-face encounters can be planned or spontaneous.

Essential Activity #70

Each day you are part of a group. Some of your groups are formal, complete with dues and bylaws; others are informal. Some are professional, others personal. The people closest to you often know the least about what you really do! Gently remind your friends, family, and associates about the benefits of parks and recreation. Seek out new groups of people in your target audiences and educate them about the benefits.

Figure 70-1 lists some common types of groups, as well as specific organizations to help guide you to the types of organizations and people in your target audience. Add your own groups and take note when (and if) they meet on a regular basis. Then, plan your networking activities and pursue the power of positive linking by attending meetings and getting involved.

This list is only a tiny sample of the tens of thousands of groups that meet around the country, in your community, and in your neighborhood.

Type of Group	Group Name	When Do They Meet?
Friends	Childhood friends College friends Business friends	
Neighbors	Current neighbors Former neighbors	
Formal Networking Clubs	NAWBO (National Association of Women's Business Owners) National Association of Female Executives Women in Management Ethnic business associations Chambers of commerce	
Service Clubs	Toastmasters Shriners Political clubs Rotary Lions Kiwanis Soroptimists	
Formal Leads Clubs	Leads clubs Le Tip International Business Alliance	
Professional and Trade	American Camp Association National Recreation and Park Association Local or state association	
Religious/ Cultural Groups	Church Synagogue	
Recreational	Clubs Group Leagues Classes Health/racquet/golf club Game groups	
Informal Groups	Golf foursomes Tennis doubles partners Poker or bridge buddies Running partners	
Hobby/Special Interest Groups/Classes	Computer clubs Community classes Book groups	
Educational Affiliations	Alumni association Sorority/fraternity PTA/PTO	
Charitable Causes or Volunteer Organizations	Volunteer center Fundraisers	

Figure 70-1. Make contacts and connections that really count.

Essential #71: Ignite Action With Promotional Rifles

Promotions are marketing rifles. They are the most effective vehicles for organizations with specific target audiences and some dollar budget. They are like powerful lightning bolts, able to ignite your customers to action.

Characteristics of a promotion:

- Very accurate
- Enables direct response
- Easy to measure effectiveness
- Varied in time and cost commitment
- Three-dimensional
- Multisensory
- Permanent

Promotions are best for:

- Business-to-business marketers
- Opening doors with gatekeepers and end users
- Continuity and theme development
- Establishing position and competitive edge
- Follow-up to initial contact
- Target marketing specialists

Promotional tools:

- Direct mail
- Promotional products delivered via:
  - Mail
  - Door-to-door
  - Delivery
- Trade publications
- Trade directories and newsletters
- Self-published newsletters
- Seminars
- Speaking engagements

- Demonstrations
- Trade shows
- Exhibits
- Flea markets
- Sampling
- Bulletin boards at places where your customers live, work, and play
- Online bulletin boards
- Yellow Pages
- Point of purchase
- Electronic messaging/on-hold message

Essential Activity #71

Almost every camp uses some form of promotional product, such as T-shirts imprinted with the camp name and logo. Literally hundreds of thousands of items are available for every budget. Promotional products, incentives and premiums are the most personal way to thank a customer, reward an employee, or promote a product, service, or business.

Promotional programs can work in conjunction with any of your current or upcoming marketing objectives to keep your name and message in front of your audience day after day, even when camp is not in session. The list changes every day as new trends, technologies and products are introduced. Search a free, live database of more than 250,000 ideas at www.advisorsmarketing.com, or use the list that follows to find the perfect permanent promotional tools for your target audience.

Promotional Product Categories

- Almanacs
- Appointment books and calendars
- Aprons
- Audiotapes
- Auto accessories
- Award programs
- Badge holders
- Bags
- Balls
- Banks
- Banners and pennants
- Barbecue accessories
- Barometers and hygrometers
- Baskets
- Beach towels
- Beauty aids
- Bells
- Belt buckles

- Beverage can holders/insulators
- Bibs
- Bicycle accessories
- Binders
- Binoculars
- Blankets
- Book covers
- Bookmarks
- Books
- Bottles
- Bowls
- Boxes
- Briefcases
- Bumper stickers
- Business card holders
- Buttons and badges
- CDs
- Calculators
- Calendars
- Calling card cases
- Cameras
- Candles and holders
- Candy
- Caps and hats
- Carafes
- Cards
- Carving boards
- Cell phones and accessories
- Ceramics
- Chairs
- Chalk boards
- Charts
- Cheering accessories
- Christmas ornaments
- Clipboards
- Clocks
- Clothing
- Coasters
- Coffee mugs
- Coffee pots
- Coin holders
- Coins, tokens and medallions
- Coloring books
- Combs
- Compact discs
- Computer accessories
- Cosmetics
- Credit cards
- Cups
- Cushions
- Cutters
- DVDs
- Date books
- Decals
- Decanters
- Decorations
- Dental floss
- Deodorizers
- Desk accessories
- Desk pen stands
- Diaries and journals
- Diaries
- Dishes
- Drinking glasses
- Easels
- Electronics
- Emery boards
- Erasers
- Eyeglass accessories
- Fanny packs
- Fans
- Figurines
- Files
- Fire starters
- Fireplace accessories
- Flags
- Flashlights
- Fly swatters
- Flying saucers and discs
- Food gifts
- Foreign language translators
- Forks and spoons
- Frames
- Fresheners
- Furniture
- Games
- Gift cards
- Gift wrap

- Glass specialties
- Globes
- Gloves
- Goggles
- Golf accessories
- Hair dryers
- Headbands
- Highlighters
- Hooks
- Horns
- Ice buckets
- Index cards
- Jackets
- Jar openers
- Jewelry
- Key cases
- Key holders
- Key tags
- Knives
- Labels
- Laminating machines and supplies
- Lapel pins
- Leather goods
- Leis
- Letter openers
- License plate frames
- License plates
- Lighters
- Lint removers
- Lip balm
- Lotions
- Loving cups and trophies
- Magnets
- Magnifiers
- Maps and atlases
- Masks
- Massagers
- Matchbooks
- Mats
- Measures
- Medals
- Memo boards
- Memo pad and paper holders
- Memo pads and books
- Metal cast items
- Miniatures and replicas
- Mirrors
- Mitts
- Money converters/foreign exchange calculators
- Money novelties
- Mugs and steins
- Musical specialties
- Nameplates
- Napkin rings and holders
- Napkins
- Newsletters
- Noisemakers
- Organizers
- Page protectors
- Pails and buckets
- Paper clips
- Paperweights
- Party favors
- PDAs (personal digital assistants) and accessories
- Pen and pencil sets
- Pen and pencil holders
- Pencil cases
- Pencils
- Pens
- Pepper mills
- Perfumes and colognes
- Phone indexes
- Phones
- Photo albums
- Picnic coolers
- Pillows
- Pitchers
- Place mats
- Plaques
- Plastic cards
- Plates

- Playing cards
- Pocket protectors
- Polishers
- Portfolios
- Postcards
- Pot holders
- Potpourri burners and holders
- Puzzles and tricks
- Radios
- Rattles
- Razors
- Recycled products
- Reflectors
- Ribbon
- Ring binders
- Rulers
- Rolodex™ cards
- Sachets
- Scarves
- Scrapers
- Sewing kits
- Shirts
- Shoehorns
- Shoelaces
- Shoes
- Shovels
- Signs and displays
- Slide guides, information guides

- Snacks
- Soap
- Sponges and sponge holders
- Spoons and spoon rests
- Sport bags
- Stained glass
- Stands
- Staple removers
- Stationery
- Stockings
- Stopwatches
- Straps
- Straws
- Stuffed animals
- Sunscreen
- Sunglasses
- Sweatshirts
- Sweaters
- T-shirts
- Tags
- Tape
- Tape measures
- Tattoos (temporary)
- Thermometers
- Tiaras and crowns
- Ties
- Timers

- Tins
- Tire gauges
- Tools and hardware
- Tools, kitchen
- Toothbrushes
- Toothpicks
- Tops and spinners
- Tote bags
- Towels
- Towelettes
- Toys
- Travel mugs
- Umbrellas
- Uniforms
- Utility clips
- Vases
- Vests
- Visors
- Wallets
- Wands and scepters
- Watches
- Water bottles
- Whistles
- Wine
- Wine chillers
- Wristbands
- Yo-yos

Essential #72: Get the Word out With Publicity and Public Relations

Publicity is a powerful tool for marketers who learn to use it properly. Publicity refers to free space and time given to businesses in exchange for information, education, and news. It also refers to the image you create in the community and with your various "publics."

Characteristics of publicity:

- Free
- Accuracy varies
- Difficult to control
- Time commitment required to write news releases and build media relationships
- Dollar commitment if a firm is hired to generate publicity
- No guarantees

Publicity works best for:

- Establishing credibility
- Increasing awareness
- Announcing unique services or products
- Supporting other marketing vehicles
- Establishing position and a competitive edge
- Those with writing skills or the budget to employ a skilled publicist

Publicity possibilities:

- News releases to:
  - Print media
  - Broadcast media
  - Internet media
- Speaking to nonprofit groups
- Interviews on radio and television programs
- Charitable contributions
- Team sponsorships
- Community and political involvement

Essential Activity #72

Using the template in Figure 72-1, write a press release to publicize your camps. Focus on a benefit or solution that your camp offers that readers may not be familiar with. Send the press release to media outlets in conjunction with National Sign Your Child Up for Camp Day.

[Date]

For Immediate Release
For More Information, Call:
[Name]
[Phone number]

Headline [Tells editors about the solution or benefit]

Dateline (Your City, State)—The lead paragraph must grab their attention. It should be interesting factual, statistical, and intriguing, and remind editors of the readers' problem.

Body—Use subheadings and subtitles to break down your subject matter into small, related chunks that are easy to read and skim.

Don't forget to use quotes. It's the most effective way to make you sound like a credible expert.

Transitional words and phrases make a news release flow:

- Another reason
- Besides
- Even though
- Therefore
- The second way is
- Similarly
- In the same way

- Yet
- But
- However
- On the other hand
- And in addition to
- Next

Call to action—Always ask your reader to "do something" as a result of reading your news release. The call to action is the only place in the news release where you should sound like you are "selling" anything.

###

Close your press release with either "###" or "-30-", both of which signify the end of your piece. The symbol should be centered at the bottom of the page.

Figure 72-1. Essential press release format

Essential #73: Reach the Masses With Mass Media Advertising

Mass media acts as a marketing shotgun because it can hit a broad target with a lesser degree of accuracy. Shotguns should only be used by marketers who are truly trying to appeal to the masses. Those marketers aiming for a small, narrow target are better off sticking to rifles and laser beams.

Characteristics of mass media shotguns:

- Inaccurate
- Reach the masses
- Allows for quick response
- Relatively expensive in terms of dollars
- Difficult to measure the effectiveness of electronic media
- Coupons provide an easy way to measure the effectiveness of print media
- High degree of wasted exposure
- Lots of clutter
- Can be multisensory

Mass media is best for:

- Consumer marketers with a wide target
- Those with little time, but lots of dollars to invest

Examples of mass media shotguns:

- Newspapers
- Network television
- Cable television (can be a rifle depending upon program audience)
- Radio
- Magazines
- Outdoor/transportation
- Widely distributed direct mail
- Mass email

Mass media advertising is good for reaching large numbers of people, but it can be costly.

Essential Activity #73

Tune in to the TV programs and radio stations that appeal to your target audience. Read the magazines, newspapers, or websites that your target audiences read. Jot down all of the advertisers that you hear and see. Look at the list and ask yourself the following questions:

- Does my organization fit alongside these advertisers?

- Do local or targeted alternatives exist that might be more affordable for my camps?

Essential #74: Use Media Reps

Many advertising and promotional vehicles are sold by media representatives or account executives who will gladly educate you about local media options either in person or over the telephone. Never, however, waste anyone's time with misleading questions and false promises. Instead, honestly explain that you are learning about different media options in your quest to build a complete marketing strategy.

The best way to find professional media assistance is to ask your network of contacts for recommendations. If your contacts are unable to help, consider these methods:

- Chamber of commerce

- Trade and professional associations

- Direct contact with media

- Business-to-business telephone directories; consider these categories:

  - Advertising agencies
  - Advertising specialties
  - Marketing
  - Radio stations
  - Newspapers
  - Packaging
  - Graphic artists

Media representatives are a wealth of knowledge, but they have their own sales agenda. Use them wisely and they can become great partners.

Essential Activity #74

Choose a newspaper, radio station, website, or other form of media that appeals to your target audience.

■ First, use the Internet to gather as much information as possible about what it costs to advertise on that media.

■ Then make a call to a salesperson representing that media to gather additional information about media rates and feasibility.

■ Specifically find out how much it would cost to air your commercial or place an ad in a newspaper, magazine, newsletter, or website.

■ Ask that a rate card be sent to you. Once received, review the information on the rate card.

■ After talking to your sales representative, answer the following questions:

- What advice does the ad rep give?
- How many times does the ad rep recommend your commercial airs or ad runs to best reach your target audience?
- Does the media rep stay objective? Do you think he or she had your best needs in mind? Do you feel that you can completely trust the advice of this sales rep? Why or why not?
- Don't be afraid to make a follow-up call to the ad rep to clarify points of information that you do not understand.

Essential #75: Stay in Control of Your Marketing

While most media and promotional reps are professional, beware! Bigger is not always better. Most salespeople earn their income on commission. It is in their pocketbook's best interest to sell you more than you may need. Never let a salesperson steer you away from your marketing plan. It is your map. Don't let anyone lead you astray.

By using your marketing plan as your blueprint, along with your target audience's input, you can stay in control of your media expenditures. Work with media reps to help you test their media without committing to long schedules and contracts. However, don't give up without giving your vehicle a fair chance to work. It may take several exposures of your message to get the action you want.

Use your marketing plan to stay in control of your decisions. When in doubt, get customer input.

Essential Activity #75

Before making your final decision about advertising through a particular medium, call a noncompetitor who is currently advertising in that form of media. Be very gracious and thank them for their time as you conduct some marketing research. Most businesspeople will be happy to help.

- Find out how well this form of advertising has worked for them.

- Ask them how often their ad runs and if they have any advice or suggestions to increase your results.

Essential #76: Take the Final Test Before Your Invest

It's clear that many ways are available to reach your customers and prospects. To work, each and every promotion must do the following:

- Meet your target customer's needs, wants, and desires
- Be timed for results
- Break through your customer's clutter
- Stimulate and motivate the recipient to buy or act now

This checklist will help ensure that your marketing works!

Essential Activity #76

Before you complete your promotional process, make a final check to ensure that you haven't missed something essential.

Warning! For your promotion to work, you must answer "yes" to at least one question in each of the four categories in the following checklist. The more "yes" answers, the greater your chances of success.

Promotion Checklist

■ What's in it for them?

- Was your promotion created specifically for your target audience?
- Does your promotion address the problems or questions facing your specific target audience?
- Does your promotion clearly show, state, or tell how you solve your target audience's problems?

■ Perfect timing

- Will your specific target audience see your promotion at the time they are ready to buy?
- Is your promotion permanent or does it have lasting power? Will your specific target audience be able to find or see your promotion at the time they are ready to buy?

- Will your prospect remember your promotion, product, or service when they're ready to buy?

■ Clutter busters

- Does your promotion cause the recipient to stop, look, or listen?
- Does your promotion create curiosity or have shock value?
- Is your promotion multisensory? Does it involve more than one of the recipient's senses (i.e., sight, smell, touch, hearing, and taste)?
- Is your promotion interactive? Does it allow your customer to get involved?

■ Motivate and stimulate action

- Does your promotion request or require immediate response or action?
- Does your promotion create a sense of urgency?
- Does your promotion provide a response mechanism or make it simple for the customer to act or buy from you?

8

Get Physical with On-Site Marketing

"Be a yardstick of quality. Some people aren't used to an environment where excellence is expected."
—Steve Jobs

Think about all of the properties and places that your agency owns, operates, leases, maintains, or occupies. Whether you manage camps or other facilities, parks, or open space, you have countless opportunities to communicate to your customers and visitors—right on site! One of the least expensive, yet most effective, ways to market your message is to take advantage of your physical spaces and places.

Essential #77: Take a Customer Stroll

The simplest way to get a sense of your on-site marketing effectiveness is to imagine and experience what it feels like to be a customer. In many cases, camp or recreation staff members enter and exit buildings and facilities using a designated "staff" entrance, causing them to lose customer perspective. It's easy to regain the focus you need by taking an informal journey. This journey is not meant to be a meticulous, clipboard-in-hand investigation. Rather, it is meant to give you an overview of the customer experience. Future Essentials will allow you to gain additional details and information.

When was the last time you walked through your facilities along the same path as a typical customer? When was the last time you drove into your facility fully aware of its curb appeal and physical appearance? In other words, when was the last time you followed in the footsteps (and tire tracks) of a typical customer?

When customers enter your parking lot, do they feel encouraged and excited about being there? Or do they see things that are broken or in some state of disarray?

Enter your facility through the customer door. What do you see? If you didn't know where you were going, are clear directions available to help you find your way? Continue on your journey while wearing your customer hat. Visit the restrooms and waiting areas. Imagine that you are lost for a while. How easy is it to get back on the right course?

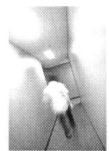

Do customers feel welcomed and warm or lost and alone?

Essential Activity #77

After you have taken the customer stroll, ask yourself:

• Would I be willing to entrust my child to this organization knowing what I know about the way they care for their facilities? What would have to be different to give me complete confidence in this organization and its staff?

Essential #78: Promote With POP

Look around your facility. Take a walk through your camps. Drive up and down your main streets. Take a walk through your mega-mall. Notice the messages, ads, words, and images. Everywhere you look, someone is trying to tell you something. Sometimes messages are subtle—almost invisible. Other times the messages visually scream at you like something out of a promotional horror film.

Strategic on-site marketing is known as POP (point of purchase). As a camp, you can think of your POP as both the place customers might visit to register or gather information about your camps as well as the *point of participation.* Of course, your point of participation varies based on the type of camp you offer, from a traditional residential camp facility to a museum, theme park, or sports field. While you never want to clutter your environment with unsightly propaganda, you do want to capitalize on on-site opportunities to educate, inform, and encourage customers to take action.

You currently post all kinds of information throughout your agency—hours, rules, directions, instructions, identification, schedules, and more. Walls, floors, kiosks, trailheads, distance markers, bulletin boards, and interior and exterior signs can help customers, campers, and staff members feel good about being part of your organization.

Essential Activity #78

Look around your camps, paying particular attention to your existing POP (Point of Purchase) marketing. Take a walk through your offices or your campsite and look for the following:

- Posters, signs, pictures, artwork, doormats, certificates, murals, benches, trailheads, athletic fields, pools, classrooms, studios, and other points of participation

- Décor, or lack thereof

- Do you have counter cards, napkins, cups, brochures, bulletin boards, brochure racks, floors, walls, banners, or marquees?

- Make a list of places where you might be able to add some promotional pizzazz.

- Work with camp counselors or art teachers to create art projects with a promotional message that could be tastefully and strategically displayed throughout your facilities.

Essential #79: Engage All of the Senses

When customers phone, drive by, or set foot in your facility, offices, and camps they see, hear, feel, smell, and even taste your quality, value, and personality. Each customer encounter is a chance for you to reinforce their decision to do business with you. If, however, a parent or child visits your camps, offices, or other facilities and things don't feel or look safe, secure, and inviting, you may cause buyer's remorse or anxiety, or even send them away forever.

Take another walk around your agency or facility. Visit the classrooms, gym, playground, pool, or nature trails. What do you *see*? Children running? Senior citizens ballroom dancing? Signs? Litter? Is your facility well-lit or is it dark and gloomy? How's the *temperature*?

Listen to the *sounds* of your facilities. What do you hear? Children laughing, staff yelling, birds chirping, leaves rustling, water splashing, or balls bouncing? *Taste* the water in your drinking fountains and nibble on the snacks in the after-school classrooms. Take a deep breath and *smell* the aromas. Do you smell freshly cut grass, popcorn, chlorine, or sweat? *Touch* and feel your way around. Sit in the chairs. Are they comfortable?

Temperature, lighting, and litter—It would be impossible to talk about creating a customer-centered atmosphere without mentioning these things. Do you regularly walk your facility to make sure it is free of hazards and litter? Any facility boasting benefits must be safe and secure for staff and participants.

Everyone wants to be comfortable. No matter how brilliant your programs or how professional your staff, if people are too cold, that may be all they remember. Is it too cold, too hot, or just right?

Any electrician or interior designer will tell you that lighting is one of the most important ways to create mood and atmosphere in any space. Lighting that is too dim or harsh can become an obstacle to participation. Softball can't be played in the dark. Quilters can't work in low lighting. Lights that buzz or flicker will soon annoy visitors and staff alike. People will stay in the dark about the benefits if they aren't well lit.

Music and sound—Noise and sound continuously creep into people's conscious and subconscious minds. Make sure your buildings' acoustics and phone systems enable good sound and communication between customers and staff. In addition, when using sound systems to make announcements, make sure all necessary participants can easily hear. Nothing is more disappointing than missing an event or contest because sound systems were inadequate.

Some children and adults are more sensitive to noise than others. Unpleasant or loud noises can transform an otherwise perfect situation into one that is intolerable. On the other hand, carefully chosen music adds wonderful ambience to every situation. What kind of music can be played throughout your facility? What kind of music can be played in reception areas, cabins, studios, dining areas, etc.?

Familiarize yourself with music licensing requirements. The American Society of Composers, Authors, and Publishers (ASCAP) website is a good place to begin your education (www.ascap.com).

Refreshments—Can you serve refreshments to visitors? While it may not be feasible to serve tea and crumpets on a regular basis, it may be possible to place a candy dish at your information counter. During hot summer months, make sure there's plenty of drinking water throughout your facilities.

On high-traffic days, consider serving lemonade, coffee or other inexpensive beverages to patrons forced to wait in lines. All of these extras enhance the customer's experience at your facility, creating an atmosphere where your image can thrive. Work with local food and beverage distributors, retailers, or coffee houses who may want to use your facilities as a place to sample new products or meet potential customers.

Smell of success—Your facility is a multisensory smorgasbord of smells, sights, sounds, and tastes. Just like a restaurant's ambience can be stuffy, festive, casual, or happy, your facilities radiate mood—positive or negative.

For example, you may offer an evening orientation aimed at helping young children get over the anxiety of going to camp for the very first time. Unfortunately, the room where your orientation is scheduled to take place is also used as an art studio and smells of cleaning chemicals from an earlier activity. Children, especially those sensitive to harsh odors, could associate your camp with the bad smells and feel more anxious than ever.

As you walk through your facilities, tune in to all of your senses.

Essential Activity #79

As you take one last walk through your facilities, digging deeper into the sensory experience. Rather than focusing on typical observations, stretch your senses and notice smells, subtle visual cues, and the sounds beneath the sounds. Sit in the chairs and on the benches to feel how comfortable they are. Look behind chairs and couches. Taste the food and drink from the water fountains. Is the water cold? Is the food flavorful?

- What can you do immediately to improve the physical experience for your customers and staff?

- What changes would you like to make in the future?

- Keep all five senses—smell, sight, hearing, taste, touch—in mind as you make your list.

Essential #80: Rate Your Place

The previous few activities have given you a chance to get a general sense of your facility's physical strengths and weaknesses. By creating a more formal assessment, you can ensure ongoing on-site marketing success.

Formal assessments ensure consistent standards of excellence.

Essential Activity #80

Although every camp, facility, and organization is different, certain things are universal when evaluating your on-site marketing effectiveness.

- Use Figure 80-1 to systematically gather initial information about your physical image and quality.

- Add additional criteria to reflect your camp's features (e.g., include special amenities such as pools, chapels, dining halls, etc.).

- Make improvements where necessary.

- Re-evaluate on a regular basis (daily, weekly, monthly, or quarterly).

Essential On-Site Evaluation

	Poor	Adequate	Excellent	Comments
Exterior Entrance				
Signage				
Curb appeal				
Neighborhood				
Cleanliness				
Freedom from hazards				
Interior				
Cleanliness				
Clutter				
Lighting				
Smell				
Signage				
Decor				
Safety				
General maintenance				
Initial Staff Encounter				
Prompt				
Greetings				
Easily identified				
Knowledgeable				
Waiting Areas				
Comfortable				
Stimulating/ entertaining				
Convenient				
Restrooms				
Cleanliness				
Well-stocked				
On-site Promotional Materials				
Useful for visitor				
Easy to access				
Well organized				
Neat				
Exit				
Signage				
Cleanliness				
Shows appreciation				

Figure 80-1. On-site evaluation

Essential #81: Win the Waiting Game

Have you ever found yourself reading incredibly outdated magazines or newspapers while waiting for your doctor or dentist? Waiting customers are often especially hungry for something to keep themselves occupied or entertained.

- Create a crossword, word search, or other word puzzle that uses clues related to your organization or camp. Place them strategically in waiting or spectator areas. Include information about upcoming programs or future activities.

- Customer input opportunity—While customers are waiting, encourage them to fill out a survey, comment card, or opinion poll.

- For children, supply coloring books, dot-to-dot games, or simple game sheets that focus on camp-related themes. Educational coloring books about playground safety, self-esteem, fitness, diversity, and drug prevention can even be customized with your agency's name and logo (see www.advisorsmarketing.com).

- Put a DVD player or VCR in your waiting area where you can show videos about your camp, animated cartoons related to camp, or other customer-friendly entertainment.

- Create an entire library of books, videotapes, and magazines that relate to any aspect of camp, fitness, children, parenting, your community, etc. Ask other organizations such as the American Heart Association, or your local police department, chamber of commerce, sports associations, or social service agencies if they have materials that would benefit your customers. Don't forget to ask if they would be willing to distribute your information in exchange.

Take a seat—It makes good common sense that people might want to comfortably sit while waiting in your facility. Parents or grandparents can often be found sitting on a gymnasium floor while children participate in classes or games. If your agency is committed to your community's kids, you must also be committed to their chauffeurs— also lovingly known as Mom, Dad, Grandma, or Grandpa. For example, if no chairs are available where Grandpa can comfortably sit and watch while little Johnny kicks his way to his black belt, chances are that Grandpa, with his bad back and arthritis, is probably not enjoying the benefits, but rather is painfully enduring the experience.

Provide a kid-friendly environment—Is your facility kid-friendly? It should be a place where parents can safely bring children while registering for camps or future programs. No one hates waiting in line more than little kids. A five-minute wait can seem like a lifetime to a toddler.

- Can you add a small play area so children can happily entertain themselves while Mom or Dad calmly get the information they need about your products?

- Do you have drinking fountains for little kids? Can you add a stool to the adult-sized fountains you have?
- Are you able to simultaneously schedule childcare or children's programs during adult-only activities?

Waiting should not be painful.

Essential Activity #81

Send yourself to a time-out in one of your most popular waiting areas. It might be a lobby, reception area, office, or curb. Set a timer and force yourself to wait for 10 minutes.

- What did you do to pass the time?

- What could you do to help customers make better use of their waiting time?

- How can you take advantage of this down time to market future programs or opportunities to your waiting customers?

Essential #82: Dress to Impress

The way you and your staff present themselves to your customers and prospects is an integral part of your marketing success. Many of your best camp staff members are young, hip, and trendy. Their ability to relate to your campers is often the difference between a good and a great camp experience.

However, while counselors can be cool, they also must look professional and responsible. In addition, your front-line staff members are like windows reflecting your camp's quality and image. Staff uniforms are a great way to create a consistent look for your most important point-of-purchase resource—your staff.

Uniforms come in many forms, from T-shirts, collared sports shirts, and sweats to bathing suits, lab coats, and blazers. Almost anything can be screen printed or embroidered to include your camp's name, logo, or message. When choosing camp or staff uniforms or apparel, keep the following aspects in mind:

- *Professional appearance*—Coordinate colors with the facility and staff. Consider a traditional polo shirt, denim, or khakis.

- *Comfortable apparel*—Camp staff get down and dirty on a daily basis. Uncomfortable clothes create problems. Even office staff want to be comfortable as they serve customers and other staff.

- *Cost*—Low cost is not always your best value. Low-end apparel rarely takes the abuse of continual washing, making it in a poor investment.

- *Durability*—Keep in mind that higher-quality apparel gives you more for your money, as it maintains color and shape longer. In most cases, the cost difference between low-end and medium/high-end staff apparel is minimal.

- *Style*—Especially when marketing to kids, it's important to keep styles and colors current and fresh. Even older facilities come alive when staff members present an up-to-date image.

- *Employee identification*—Color and logo identification make staff easily recognizable to your campers, parents, visitors, and customers

- *Camp logo*—Putting your camp or organization logo on staff apparel makes great marketing sense. While the traditional placement has been on the front left chest, just about anything goes. Remember that staff will wear the uniform out of the facility, consequently providing additional advertising.

Uniformed staff, volunteers, and campers impress on- and off-site

Essential Activity #82

For a few days, pay particular attention to the apparel worn by the people in various work forces. From your delivery man to the supermarket clerk, almost everyone is in uniform. Log on to www.advisorsmarketing.com or www.uniforms.com to browse through thousands of options to help your staff dress for success.

Essential #83: Use Human Billboards

You've undoubtedly seen human sign-wavers standing, jumping, and dancing on street corners, promoting everything from real estate and furniture liquidations to car washes and special events. While your staff might not be ready to dance their way to marketing stardom, they can still serve as living, breathing messengers. Take staff uniforms to a new level by adding unique name tags, buttons, stickers, lapel pins, appliqués, hats, or other accessories. Consider the following ways to use on-person promotion:

- During the off-season, staff can promote registration dates by donning buttons that say, "Camp Registration Begins March 31!"

- Imprint the back of staff T-shirts to say, "Follow me to the fun!"

- Wear American Camp Association Lapel Pins to ignite conversation about accreditation.

- Wear appliqués or Weepuls (those fuzzy, pom characters such as those pictured below) to promote specialty camps. These fun, stick-on items can be customized in hundreds of ways to represent just about any camp you offer. Staff members can wear them on their shoulders or name badges. They can adorn your counters or computers. No matter where these irresistible critters sit, they are sure to spark great conversation.

Humans are great marketers and can show and tell your story.

Essential Activity #83

Go to your favorite mall and look at all of the ways retailers use on-person promotion to help you make buying decisions. Write down at least five ideas you might be able to incorporate into your marketing plan.

Essential #84: Make Goodbyes Great

You never get a second chance to make a first impression. But, you also never get a better place to leave a great lasting impression than at the point of departure. Camp goodbyes come in many forms. From the final farewell of the season to a daily day-camp drop-off, your customers "leave" your facilities using many modes of transportation. Some leave your facilities and board planes, trains, and automobiles before being reunited with family. Day campers are dropped of by parents each morning. Some customers even walk to your facilities.

Whether parents drop off their children once a year or each and every day, what do they see as they exit your buildings and drive away? Do campers feel rushed out the door as the staff celebrates the end of work or are campers shown appreciation and gratitude? Even the most emotional goodbye can become an opportunity for you to reinforce the buying decision, instill confidence in your staff, or show appreciation.

Camp goodbyes can be bittersweet. Give a lasting award, reward, or gift of thanks as campers and staff say farewell.

Essential Activity #84

Work with staff to create an exit strategy that exceeds your customers' expectations. Encourage staff to walk and drive the same path as parents and campers to get a true sense of what it feels, looks, and sounds like for:

- Customers to leave your offices or registration facilities

- Parents to say "goodbye" to children

- Campers to say "goodbye" to friends, counselors, staff, and the overall camp experience

9

More Than a Feeling—Elevate Your Emotional Atmosphere

"Do more than is required. What is the distance between someone who achieves their goals consistently and those who spend their lives and careers merely following? The extra mile."
—Gary Ryan Blair

How does it feel to be your customer? Do your customers feel like royal guests or are they treated as annoying interruptions? Creating a customer-centered environment is as much about the emotional atmosphere as it is about the physical atmosphere. In addition, ongoing input and feedback are crucial to ensure that you are meeting the needs of your customers, campers, and parents.

Essential #85: Take the Customer Care Quiz

Do you have what it takes to effectively work with people, even when they are at their worst? While everyone can have a bad day once in a while, it's important to assess both your natural and acquired abilities when it comes to customer care.

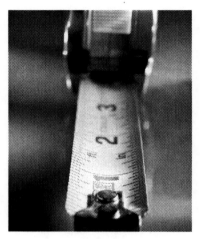

As a customer care specialist, how do you measure up?

Essential Activity #85

After completing the Essential Customer Care Quiz presented in Figure 85-1 and evaluating your results, ask yourself the following questions:

- What could I do in the next 30 days to improve my score?

- What type of training could I explore to help me better serve my customers?

- Which of these obstacles might be altered to better serve the customers?

Essential Customer Care Quiz

		4	3	2	1	0
		Always	Most of the Time	Some-times	Seldom	Never
1.	I feel good about myself.					
2.	I feel knowledgeable about my job and my agency.					
3.	I talk about the quality of my camps or organization with customers and co-workers.					
4.	I love working with people.					
5.	I enjoy solving problems.					
6.	I work well under pressure.					
7.	I can easily juggle many projects at once.					
8.	I handle interruptions with ease.					
9.	I adapt easily to new situations.					
10	I believe that the customer is the most important person in my agency.					
11.	I feel empowered to handle customer problems on my own.					
12	I take criticism well.					
13.	When talking on the telephone, I smile and am enthusiastic.					
14	I feel committed to my job and my agency.					
15.	I greet people when they enter my facility/office/area/etc.					
16	When I don't know the answer to a customer's question, I quickly find the answer and follow-up with the customer.					
17.	My work area is neat and organized.					
18	I take pride in my appearance and know that I represent my agency.					
19.	I follow-up with customers after they have complained.					
20	I speak highly of my agency.					
21.	I speak highly of my co-workers, supervisors, managers, and decision-makers.					
	Total Each Column					

Figure 85-1. Customer care quiz

Self-Test Scores

Add up the number of answers in each column and total your points as follows:
- 4 points for each "Always."
- 3 points for each "Most of the Time"
- 2 points for each "Sometimes"
- 1 point for each "Seldom"
- 0 points for "Never"

75–84	**Congratulations! You are a "customer service superhero." Your attitude is contagious. Share your enthusiasm with others.**
51–74	**Good job! You have all the right stuff to deliver "amazing customer service." Consistency is the key to reaching superstardom.**
36–50	You're on your way. Take a deep breath and focus on the customers' needs. Work with your supervisor to make sure that you are getting the necessary support to skillfully communicate with customers.
22–35	While you may not love working with people, it is a necessary part of every job. Take small steps to improve your attitude by constructively discussing issues with supervisors and co-workers.
0–21	Yikes. This score indicates poor self-confidence, job dissatisfaction, and a complete lack of customer-service skills. For now you may be better off working behind the scenes.

Figure 85-1. Customer care quiz (cont.)

Essential #86: Become a Customer Service Super Model

The level of customer service often directly reflects the level of respect that managers show to staff members. Amazing customer service occurs only when managers treat their staff as valuable customers, too. Frederick Smith, Chairman and CEO of Federal Express, said it best when he remarked, "Customer satisfaction begins with employee satisfaction."

In addition, managers must be shining examples of exceptional customer service. They should not ask staff to perform a task that they would not be willing to do themselves. No one who works for your camp is too good or important to pick up litter, answer a phone, or help a customer find his way.

Lead your team to great customer care through enthusiastic example. They will treat customers as they are treated.

Essential Activity #86

Answer the following questions as honestly as possible. Bring your managers together to discuss these questions and commit to becoming better role models for your staff.

- Do you treat your staff the way you want your staff to treat your customers? If not, what can you do to improve your "internal customer service"?

- In what ways do you model amazing customer service for your staff?

- How could you be a better model?

Essential #87: Hire People Personalities

When recruiting and hiring staff for your camp, depending upon the position, you may require applicants to have professional certifications, licenses, or degrees. However, you also should be looking for staff members who truly enjoy working with people and solving their problems. In other words, you can't train personality.

Hire people who love people. You can't train personality.

Essential Activity #87

Adapt the customer care quiz (see Figure 85-1) as part of your application process to determine whether candidates have what it takes to deal with all types of customers.

Essential #88: Train the Entire Team

Every person that comes in contact with your customer, no matter how briefly, is part of your customer service and marketing team. Even concessionaires, volunteers, contractors, and temporary staff can make or break customer relationships. Stress the importance of customer service during job interviews and when developing agreements with independent contractors. When you consider the cost of advertising and attracting new customers to your camps, one of the best investments you can make is high-quality customer service training for everyone on your team.

Professional customer service workshops may be less expensive than you think, especially when compared to the high cost of lost revenue due to poor service. You can also explore other training tools such as videos, online webinars, and audiotapes. Of course, your local libraries and bookstores have shelves of books and other resources to help elevate customer service skills.

Make it your job to help everyone in your organization become part of your marketing success. Create an ongoing training system to ensure that all staff members treat customers like royalty, rather than like an inconvenience. Review the following ways to ensure amazing customer service:

- Internal staff training
- External seminars and workshops
- Staff meetings
- New customer-centered job descriptions
- A company mission statement
- Rewards for exceptional service
- Suggestion programs
- Additional staff
- Delegating of tasks that get in the way of customer service
- Communicating of customer-service goals with everyone

Create a consistent standard of service for everyone on your team, including those working behind the scenes. Everyone impacts the customer experience. "Together Everyone Achieves More."

Essential Activity #88

Many ways exist to bring customer service education to your staff. From professional workshops to on-the-spot coaching, make a commitment to help your team better serve your campers and customers. Log on to www.advisorsmarketing.com to explore over 70 workshop ideas.

What three things will you do to nurture customer service excellence from yourself and everyone on your team?

- _____
- _____
- _____

Essential #89: Be Easy to Buy From

Nothing seems more basic, but sometimes it's hard to be a customer. Your registration process might be cumbersome, complete with long lines and longer forms. Most people want to plan recreation activities from the comfort of their computers. Online registration is the state of the art.

When it comes to your hours of operation, are the dates and times more convenient for staff or for customers? Consider these examples:

- Your summer specialty camps are held Monday through Friday from 9 a.m. to 12 noon. Those hours are perfect for stay-at-home moms, but what about those kids whose parents work during the day? They will never know the joys of cooking or science camp.

- "Mommy and Me" classes are typically offered mornings during the traditional work week. What a shame for those working Mommies (and Daddies, too) who would benefit from these interactive experiences.

- After-school activities, designed to enrich kids in a safe environment when parents are not home, are usually offered Monday through Friday. Seldom, however, are these types of supervised programs offered on weekends and holidays when school is also out of session. Yet, some parents work weekends and even on holidays, leaving latchkey children home alone.

As far as payments go, electronic banking is not a trend; it's part of most people's everyday lives. Many people don't carry checks anymore and rely on check cards and credit cards to pay for everything from gas to summer camp. Accept all payment options.

Public agencies, nonprofit organizations, and faith-based camps often have a mission to serve all members of their communities, regardless of their income. Do you offer assistance to economically challenged patrons so that everyone has equal access to your benefits?

Essential Activity #89

Think about your systems and processes. Name three things that you can do to make it easier for your customers to do business with you.

- _____

- _____

- _____

Essential #90: Commit to Amazing Customer Service

Amazing customer service goes beyond the ordinary to delightfully surprise and surpass customer expectations. Train your staff to understand that customer encounters must not be looked at as individual experiences, but rather the opportunity to build lifelong relationships.

Each and every person who works in a customer-centered organization must see themselves as more than their job description. Instead, each person who wears your uniform—literally or figuratively—must be trained as an ambassador for your entire agency. The guidelines that follow list seven easy ways to create a consistent culture of customer care. Post the guidelines throughout your facility to let every staff member know that the customer comes first.

Ignorance is definitely not bliss when it comes to customer service! Teach staff where to find information that their customers may need, even if it's not their department. Empower staff to think for their customers based on their own experience. Even though they may have answered a customer's questions 325 times before, remind staff that it's the first time that customer has inquired. Also, encourage staff to make suggestions regarding customer service by explaining that their perspective is priceless.

Customer Service Guidelines

Reach out:

- Welcome people immediately.
- Acknowledge customers' presence. Don't ever let anyone feel "invisible." Nothing is worse than feeling lost or ignored in a strange place. Also, people who feel invisible may do things that are inappropriate, unsafe, or destructive.
- When helping others on the phone or in person, make eye contact and smile as guests arrive.

Be friendly:

- If you are unsure if someone needs help, ask him.
- Share information willingly, even if it's "not your department."
- If you can't help, find someone who can.
- Be familiar with the programs you offer at your center and around the city.
- Smile (again)! It warms hearts and attitudes.

Be timely:

- Respond quickly.
- Explain delays.
- Always follow-up with customers as requested.

Listen actively:

- Give the customer your full attention.
- Listen to what is said.
- Take notes if you need to remember details.

Show courtesy:

- Put yourself in the other person's place.
- Be polite and helpful, and smile when helping customers in person and on the phone.
- Remember to say goodbye and thank you.

Be professional:

- Avoid using slang words or offensive/inappropriate language.
- You are part of the camp team. Represent it well!

Take pride in your appearance and your environment:

- If appropriate, wear your designated uniform.
- Be sure that your uniform is clean and free from rips, holes, and graffiti.
- Your work area is a reflection of the camp's quality. Keep it clean.

Reinforce benefits:

- Ask for customer input. "How could we be better at meeting your needs?" "What did you get out of this program/event/visit?"
- Constantly look for ways to better serve the needs of your customers.
- Use your customer comment journal to capture ideas and suggestions (see Essential #94).

Essential Activity #90

Obstacles often get in the way of delivering amazing customer service.

- Brainstorm a list of the policies, procedure, rules, systems, etc., that might be getting in the way of creating the perfect customer experience.

- Which of these obstacles might be altered to better serve the customer?

Essential #91: Expect Conflict—Give Guidelines, Empower Excellence

Is the customer always right? Not exactly, but the customer is the boss and must always be treated like a valued guest. Customer comments come in many forms, including suggestions, compliments, complaints, comments, and disputes. View customer complaints as valuable feedback. It's the job of you and your staff to handle each and every comment with grace and dignity. When training staff, especially those who are young or inexperienced, offer guidelines to help them become Customer Service H.E.R.O.S. (Figure 91-1). Empower staff to use common sense when dealing with difficult or frustrated customers.

Conflict is inevitable. Expect, train, and plan for it.

Essential Activity #91

Think back to the last time when you, as a customer, were dissatisfied, unhappy, or disgruntled. How can you use your own perspective as less-than-satisfied customer to better handle customer complaints?

- Did you "complain" to anyone? If not, why?

- If you did communicate your displeasure or frustration, how was your problem handled?

- Do you continue to give your business to this company?

H.E.R.O.S. Guide to Customer Care

Hear Everything	Keep calm.	• Two angry people are *never* more effective than one angry person. You are the person in control of the situation. Don't take the comments personally.
	Don't interrupt.	• Let him vent. In 80 percent of all conflicts, the customer just wants to be heard. He wants to know that you think his opinion is valuable. He may or may not be seeking action, and is possibly just seeking information or a "shoulder to cry on."
	Listen actively.	• If you're helping another customer, acknowledge the "angry customer" and politely tell him that you will give him your undivided attention as soon as you are finished. Use common sense. Forcing a person to wait, whether angry or not, will almost always elevate stress and anxiety. • If you are doing paperwork, put the paperwork aside! The customer always comes first. • An on-site customer takes precedent over a phone customer. • Give nonverbal cues to let the person know that you are listening, such as nodding your head. • Maintain eye contact with the customer. • Take notes if you intend to pass the information along to others. • Listen for what the customer might *not* be saying so that you can clarify later.
Reiterate	Give a positive ego message.	• Thank them for their input regarding this complaint. • If appropriate, say something like, "I totally understand how you feel. I have kids, too." Don't place or accept blame without having all the facts from all sides of the story.
	Clarify and restate the problem.	• An angry customer often will go off on unrelated tangents or include unnecessary details in his complaints. Try to restate the problem as concisely as possible. Make sure the customer agrees with your assessment of his problem.
Offer Solutions	Discuss possible solutions.	• This moment is the heart of all customer conflicts. Often you have already solved the problem—they just wanted to vent! • They may also want more. Engage their help to find a solution.
	Involve them in the solution.	• Ask, "What would you like me to do to help solve this problem?" or "Do you have any suggestions that will help us avoid this type of problem again? • Do they want a refund, a new instructor, or a discount? • Do they need to know where else they can register if a class is full? • Do they need information about your recreation council?
	Solve the problem.	• If empowered to do so, fix the problem. • If you do not have the authority to fix the problem, offer to bring the information to your manager and get back to the customer in a timely manner, or give him contact information, including hours or voicemail.
	Follow up.	• When appropriate, follow up with a phone call or note. • If you said you would call, do it! If you said you would pass the information along to your manager or recreation council, do it. • Keep the customer informed of any progress or changes caused by his suggestion. You will win a customer for life!

Figure 91-1. H.E.R.O.S. customer communication guide

Essential #92: Listen Obsessively to Your Customers

Continual input and feedback are crucial to not only your marketing, but also to your agency's future. Customers and noncustomers can all offer important ideas and insights to improve your camps and communication.

It's sometimes easy to get feedback from extremists (that is, people who either love or hate your agency). Make sure you get input from a diverse customer mix. In some cases, you may need to translate surveys and evaluations into other languages to ensure that you are getting input from non-English speakers.

It's also important to reach noncustomers as well. Noncustomers who fit your target audience profile can help you understand why people *don't* get involved with your camps or programs. Survey noncustomer targets via phone, mail, or in person. Malls and grocery stores are good places to begin. Always ask permission from off-site managers before approaching their customers.

Your ability to gather customer feedback will directly result in greater profits and success.

Essential Activity #92

Review the research methods that follow. Choose the one method that you will incorporate into your current or upcoming camp season to gain real and honest customer feedback about your camps.

Suggestion box—While low-tech and not always effective, a well-placed suggestion box is a good way to show customers and employees that their opinions matter. Make sure to attach paper and pencil so that it's easy to jot down an idea.

Web page—Like a virtual suggestion box, your website should offer a link for customers to make suggestions. Put your email and web address everywhere and let people know that you personally read and respond to every email suggestion.

Email or text message—Email and instant messaging (IM) are great communication tools. If possible, create a special hotline for IMs and a dedicated email address such as ideas@youragency.com or suggestions@youragency.com. Remember that emails and text messages must be answered in a timely manner. So, if you invite customers to email suggestions to your agency, make certain that someone is in place to respond.

On-site email—Set up a computer terminal right at your camp or in your facility where people can send you, your director, or someone else in your agency an instant message. This tool is great, especially for people who don't have email access. It offers immediacy and allows people to put suggestions or complaints in their own words in a completely anonymous forum.

Surveys—Surveys conducted via mail, telephone, email, or face-to-face can give quantitative feedback, especially if they are related to quality. For best results, keep surveys short.

Focus groups and studies—Focus-group interviews bring together customers or prospects in an informal setting to gather opinions through guided conversation with an impartial facilitator. When conducted properly, a focus group is one of the most valuable ways to gain insight into customer and noncustomer needs, wants, desires, and feelings.

Better evaluations—You may already distribute post-program evaluations to your customers. In addition to asking them about features (things like program quality, price, location, etc.), include benefits questions. The following questions can get you started:

- Would you recommend this program to others? Why or why not?
- Why did you take this program?
- What did you get out of this program?
- How did you benefit from this program?
- How did your children benefit from this program?
- Has this program helped you reduce your feelings of stress and anxiety? In what ways?
- In what ways has your health improved during the course of this program?
- Has this program helped you reach your fitness goals? In what ways?
- How has this program helped you?

Always include a "release" on evaluations, such as:

- Your comments may be used in future promotional materials.
- May we use your name and comments in future promotional materials?
  Yes No

Studies—Researchers often use studies to quantify, document, or measure the outcomes of programs and camps. For example, a study can measure whether your campers perform better in school than their noncamper peers. Or you can use a study to determine whether counselors-in-training (CITs) are more likely to become leaders in high school and college than their non-CIT peers.

Talk to them—Talk to your customers any chance you get. Or, if you never seem to get a chance, set a goal to talk casually to a certain number of customers each week or month. Visit classes, talk to fans on the ball field bleachers, work the pro shop, have lunch at the senior center, or hang out at the teen center. The idea is to engage customers in nonthreatening conversation—not to disrupt. "What did you think of the program?" "What did you get out of this program?" Look at the other sample questions in Essential Activity #93.

Measure retention—When it comes to customer satisfaction, the proof is in the "repeat business." One way to quickly and statistically gauge customer satisfaction is to measure customer retention. For example:

- What percentage of customers who registered for "Toddler Day Camp for Three Year Olds" registered the following year for "Preschool Day Camp for Four Year Olds?"
- How many of the participants of any given program have attended another program in the past?
- How many children participating in a given program have older siblings who also participated in that program?

Essential #93: Probe Deeper

Marketing research can measure everything from customer satisfaction and camp quality to marketing effectiveness and trends. Before embarking on any research project, no matter how small, take the time to clarify what information you want to gather. Then choose questions specific to your goals.

To be effective, market research must uncover both information and emotional responses.

Essential Activity #93

Read the following customer interview sample questions to begin creating your own assessment tools, marketing surveys, evaluations, and more. Consider the following as you read through the questionnaire.

- Choose the four to five questions you'd most like to ask your customers. While you might want to ask all of them, your response rate will be best if your survey is short.

- Add other questions that better fit your camp's needs.

- If you already use a survey or evaluation, add one or two of these questions to your current form.

- Create a survey or interview your customers to discover the answers you seek.

- Remember that your research can take place via phone, email, mail, on site, or in waiting areas.

Customer Interview Sample Questions

1. How did you hear about this product (program, park, facility, event, etc.)?

2. What suggestions do you have for improving this program?

3. What would happen if this program wasn't available to you?

4. How has participating or attending

   - Enhanced your life?
   - Made your life better?
   - Made your life easier?
   - Affected your health?
   - Improved your self-image?
   - Improved your skills?
   - Affected your relationships?
   - Affected your income?
   - Affected your financial well-being?

5. What suggestions do you have for other programs?

6. What kind of problems/challenges do you have that we have helped you solve?

7. What kind of problems/challenges do you have that we could help you solve?

8. What kind of problems/challenges do you have that we have helped you solve in the past?

9. What are your biggest fears?

10. What do you worry about the most?

11. What do you worry about when it comes to your children?

12. In what kind of recreation programs did you participate in the past?

13. What kind of recreation programs did you participate in when you were a child?

14. What kind of impact do you think these programs had on your life?

15. How does your participation in these programs affect the community at large?

16. How does your participation in these programs affect the economy?

17. How much money have you spent as a result of your participation in this activity?

18. How far are you willing to travel to participate in leisure activities? How far did you travel to participate in this activity?

19. How much money do you think you will spend in the next one year/five years as a result of your participation in this activity?

20. Do you think that participation in recreation or leisure activities affects your job performance or quality?

21. How have these programs affected your life?

Essential #94: Start a Customer Comment Journal

Because customer feedback often occurs during routine conversations, make it your mission to actively listen for suggestions and frustrations. Once ideas are uncovered, jot them down and make appropriate changes to better serve customer needs. Create an easy-to-use system to allow everyone on your staff, including maintenance personnel and volunteers, to capture customer comments, feedback, complaints, and ideas.

Create a customer feedback system that works for you and your staff, whether they work at a desk, in a vehicle, or outdoors.

Essential Activity #94

Create a system modeled on the customer comment journal in Figure 94-1 to make sure staff can easily capture customer input, ideas, and suggestions. Make sure journals are accessible for staff, whether they work from vehicles, outdoors, or in an office setting. While the process might seem cumbersome at first, your ability to document customer comments will greatly improve customer satisfaction.

- To encourage staff to journal comments, consider offering a reward or incentive for staff members who share the most comments during a designated period of time.

- If customers prefer, allow them to fill in comments directly into the journal themselves.

Program Area	Date	Comment	Customer's Contact Info	Action Desired By When?	Action Taken On What Date
Swimming	6/14	The water is too cold. My toddler shivers in the pool and his lips turn blue. He does not like coming to swim lessons and I'm afraid he will learn to fear the water.	Martha Spitz 123 Oak St. 555-4232 email: mspitz@xyz.net	Make the pool warmer	Beginning in September the pool will be heated to 86 degrees in the mornings for toddler and senior swim and the temperature will be lowered in the afternoon for aerobic swim. The customer was called on July 14 by Sue Smith.
Art Program	7/13	My child has burned his finger four times during art class.	Claudia Monet email: monet@abc.com	Not specified	Eliminate the use of hot glue guns in art classes for children under 8 years old or increase adult supervision during glue gun usage. Email sent by Marla (art teacher) to Ms. Monet on August 3.

Figure 94-1. Customer comment journal

10

Aftermarketing Creates Customers for Life

"Do what you do so well that customers can't help but say great things about you."
—Walt Disney

Studies show that it costs five to 10 times more to bring in a brand new customer than it does to keep the ones you already have. Why, then, is most marketing targeted to unknowns rather than to loyal customers?

Aftermarketing refers to those marketing activities that take place after a customer has made a purchase. Aftermarketing goes far beyond customer service by incorporating a whole host of proactive and ongoing communication tools. Great marketers don't just woo new customers. Instead, they keep customer allegiance alive with post-sale attention, follow-up, and added value. In this era of declining customer satisfaction and impersonal Internet transactions, it's a breeze to ignite word-of-mouth marketing with a little thoughtfulness and respect.

As a camp, your aftermarketing strategies can begin as soon as campers have registered for camp. But that's only the beginning. It's when your campers say goodbye to counselors and friends that your aftermarketing campaigns can really kick in.

To develop customers for life, you need a complete communications program. Don't spend all of your time, efforts, and money on attracting new customers. Save some of your budget to communicate with campers and alumni after their departure, throughout the year, and for the rest of their lives.

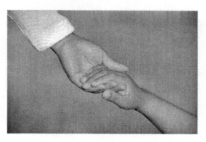

Essential #95: Calculate Your Customer Value

Your customers, campers, and counselors are the best marketing tool you have—bar none. Their personal experiences enable them to become passionate "salespeople" for you (or your competition).

- Satisfied customers may share information with friends, neighbors, co-workers, and even complete strangers.

- Delight people by going the extra mile and they become even more likely to sing your praises.

- Dissatisfied customers, while sharing negative experiences, spark debate and promote awareness and conversation.

When you lose a customer, for whatever reason, you lose the following:

- His purchase

- His lifetime purchases

- The purchases of all of his friends, relatives, neighbors, business associates, acquaintances, etc.

Essential Activity #95

It is time to get out your calculator as you determine the lifetime customer value for one of your camp customers! You're going to need it as you grasp the real value of your average customer.

- Begin this exercise by thinking of a good, but typical customer. He might be camper or parent, a retreat planner, a sponsor, an afterschool student, etc.

- Review the example in Figure 95-1 to get a sense of how customer retention multiplies over the years. Then, complete the diagram on behalf of one of your good customers.

- As you'll discover by completing the equation, each and every customer loss or loyalty adds up to much more than meets the eye.

- After you and your staff see the numbers in black and white, you may start seeing and treating your customers like the valued treasures that they are. Of course, each and every customer—even a one-time visitor—is still valuable.

The Customer Value Equation Example
Parent of One Six-Year-Old Boy
(based on a real Carlsbad, California family)

$/Time Spent Winter and Spring		$/Time Spent Summer and Fall		Annual Customer Value
$120 for Spring Break Camp $80 for Sports League $30 for Enrichment Class	**+**	$120 x five weeks of summer camp $ 70 for Sports League	**=**	$900
Annual Customer Value $900	**X**	# of years they could/ will be a customer **6 Years** (Conservative estimate based on child continuing with camps and some athletics through middle school)	**=**	**Lifetime Value** $5400
Lifetime Value $5400	**X**	Conservative # of People in "Circle of Influence" 12	**=**	**Extreme Customer Value** $64,800

The Customer Value Equation

$/Time Spent Winter and Spring		$/Time Spent Summer and Fall		Annual Customer Value
___ + ___	**+**	___ + ___	**=**	◯
Annual Customer Value ◯	**X**	# of years they could/will be a customer	**=**	Lifetime Value ☐
Lifetime Value ☐	**X**	# of People in "Circle of Influence"	**=**	Ultimate Customer Value

Figure 95-1. The customer value equation

Essential #96: Celebrate Milestones

Children of all ages love celebrating little and big personal milestones.

- As a camp, you gather a lot of personal information about your customers, including birth dates. While many adults would like to forget birthdays altogether, children count down the months, weeks, and days to their birthdays.

- Any holiday is a great day to keep in touch with your customers. Whether you want your customer to "Be Your Valentine," "Have a Spooktacular Halloween," or "Have a Bountiful Thanksgiving," use the holidays to build off-season relationships with seasonal customers.

- The end of summer vacation is the beginning of a new school year for many of your young customers and counselors. Use "Back to School" as a milestone for children. September is a great time to get parents thinking about winter camps, too.

- Educate yourself about cultural celebrations. Events such as bar and bat mitzvahs for 13-year-old Jewish children and Quinceañeras for 15-year-old Latino teens are major events.

- Faith-based camps have special opportunities to make contact during religious celebrations and holidays.

Rise above your competition by making contact and connecting to customers throughout their lives.

Essential Activity #96

Think of the last time you received an unexpected note, card, or gift in honor of a birthday, anniversary, or accomplishment. Even if the note was from a personal contact, how did it make you feel? How will you use milestone marketing to keep in touch with your campers, parents, counselors, and parents throughout the year?

Essential #97: Create a Comeback Campaign

Do you have campers or once-regular customers who seem to have fallen off the face of the earth? What happened to them? Did they:

*   Move away?

*   Get sick?

*   Burn out?

*   Go back to their couch?

*   Find a higher-quality program or product?

Comeback campaigns are a great way to touch base with misplaced customers. Let your customers know that they are missed after an absence. This tactic is especially valuable in a highly competitive environment.

Even a greeting card, handwritten note, postcard, or letter can make forgotten customers feel valued again (Figure 97-1). Consider sending camp photos or an inexpensive promotional item to inactive customers to create top-of-mind awareness, goodwill, and an invitation to return.

Figure 97-1. A comeback campaign

Essential Activity #97

More than likely, your registration system allows you to easily determine which of your campers did not come back last year. If so, do the following. If not, it's time for an upgrade!

- Create a database of these misplaced campers and reach out to them with a comeback campaign.

- At the very least, contact them to let them know they are missed and to find out what caused them to stay away. The feedback you get from previous customers may offer valuable insight into otherwise undetected program or staff issues.

Essential #98: Reward Referrals and Repeat Business

When it comes to building repeat business and generating referrals, nothing is more powerful than the quality of your camp.

- When campers have an amazing experience, they will want to return again and again. They will spread positive word-of-mouth about your fantastic camps to their friends and family.

- They may want to work for you one day.

- If you play your cards right and stay in touch with alumni throughout their lives, they may want to support you with a donation.

- Best of all, when your campers become parents, they will want to share the benefits of camping with their own children and grandchildren.

Because nothing is more valuable than a referral from a satisfied camper, parent, gatekeeper, or staff member, it makes great sense to treat referrals as precious gifts. Common courtesy dictates that you formally say "Thank you" in a meaningful and memorable way. After all, you want more referrals, don't you?

No gift is more valuable than a referral. Keep referrals coming by rewarding the behavior.

More than 100 years ago, scientists including B.F. Skinner aptly demonstrated that when you reward behavior it is sure to be repeated. Consider the following list of tools to make sure that you show appreciation for your clients, prospects, gatekeepers, and associates.

Imprinted, useful promotional products—Can be inexpensive and still have big impact. Visit www.advisorsmarketing.com to search more than 250,000 ideas.

Traditional gifts—Flowers, candy, plants, wine, etc.

Executive gifts—Can be purchased from your promotional products distributor or online from countless sources. Personalized items are especially thoughtful. Consider desk items, writing instruments, apparel, tote and sport bags, electronics, etc.

Notes—Handwritten notes are preferred.

Thank you calls—A quick call, even on voicemail is better than nothing.

Letters—Even a form letter is better than nothing.

Entertainment—Everything from movie tickets and music downloads to lunch or videos are a great way to say thanks.

Gift certificates—From your camp or organization or from a restaurant, store, or website your customer would enjoy

Merchandise—From your collection or from one of your marketing partners

Discounts on future purchases—Great gift for a frequent customer and it costs you nothing

The sky is the limit!—Something that fits your personality and position

Essential Activity #98

What kind of rewards have you received after sharing a referral with a friend, competitor, or business?

- How will you reward and show appreciation to customers, gatekeepers, and others who support your business?

- What can you do to streamline your appreciation process? Consider ordering or purchasing small gifts in bulk to ensure that referrals are rewarded promptly.

Essential #99: Create or Improve Your Post-Camp Evaluation

You may already distribute post-program evaluations to your customers or exit surveys to staff. In addition to asking them about features (program quality, satisfaction, price, location, etc.), include questions that will help you document your camps' benefits, outcomes, and value.

Always include a "release" on evaluations, such as:

- Your comments may be used in future promotional materials.

- May we use your name and comments in future promotional materials? (Yes/No)

The following questions can be edited for campers, parents, and even staff members to gain the insight you need to market and improve your programs.

- Would you recommend this camp/job to others? Why or why not?

- Why did you choose this camp/job over others?

- What did you/your child get out of this camp/job?

- How did you/your child benefit from this activity?

- Has this program helped you reduce your feelings of stress and anxiety? In what ways?

- In what ways has your child's self-esteem or social skills improved during the course of this program?

- Has this program helped you reach your fitness goals? In what ways?

- How has this program helped you?

Essential Activity #99

You must plan and dedicate yourself to developing a system to capture comments at the point of departure. Between travel plans, emotional goodbyes, and administrative duties, it's easy for end-of-camp evaluations to slip through the cracks. Remember, your chances of getting people to complete a survey greatly diminish after they have returned home.

- What will you do to capture comments from departing campers?

- What will you do to capture information and feedback from camp staff and volunteers?

- Can you make evaluations mandatory or offer an incentive?

Essential #100: Become Indispensable

Only business dinosaurs believe that you can't mix business with pleasure. You live in an era of relationship marketing. It is okay, even mandatory, to treat and support your customers as more that profit centers.

- *Friendship*—Don't give friendship in relation to the size of the person's budget.

- *Personal support*—If clients experience personal dilemmas and you can help with actions, words, or thoughts, by all means do it!

- *Information and articles*—If you see an article that might be of particular interest to a colleague, why not pop it in the mail with a quick note. An online article is easily forwarded with a click of the mouse. The effort is minimal and the thoughtfulness memorable.

- *Support their causes*—If something is important to your customer, then it should be important to you. Give generously of your time and money because of benevolence, not because of expectation. You'll feel great and so will they.

- *Become a talent scout*—You're not the only one looking for great staff. Keep your ears and eyes open, and when a vacancy occurs at a partner's or sponsor's company, you can help by referring qualified applicants to them. Your great seasonal staff might be a great addition to someone else's team when your camps aren't in session.

- *Referrals*—What goes around comes around. Give your customers referrals every chance you get and they are sure to repay the favor.

- *Resources*—Don't keep all of the great contacts to yourself. When appropriate, share the name of your super-efficient printer, graphic designer, computer technician, or day care center. It shows your customers that you are in tune with their needs.

Essential Activity #100

Building relationships and friendships can take time. Choose one person with whom you'd like to build a stronger relationship.

- Jot down three things you can do to support this person over the next few months.

- Follow through with your ideas and watch the friendship bloom.

11

Resources

"Knowledge is power."
—Sir Francis Bacon

When it comes to marketing, you will always have something more to learn—from a brand new communication tool to an emerging trend. Essential #101, while the last in this book, is certainly not the final stop on your marketing journey. The resources listed on the pages that follow represent the tens of thousands of places where you can find information and ideas to further your marketing confidence and competence. Remember, marketing information is also all around you in the form of articles, books, television programs, classes, movies, websites, audio recordings, conferences, and trade associations. As a marketer, you can never stop learning—about your competition, marketplace, media, and, of course, your customers.

Essential #101: Never Stop Learning

Turn on the television, listen to the radio, walk the aisles of your local supermarket, rent a movie, read the paper, visit your library, log on to the Internet, and talk to strangers. You can never ask too many questions when it comes to marketing. Most successful marketers have a natural sense of curiosity and wonder. When it comes to gathering information, quantity is not the goal. Instead, it's your ability to look at information—almost any information—and figure out how it applies to your products, customers, and camps. The marketer looks at the world and asks, "How does this affect me? How does this affect my customers? How can I use this information to improve my programs and make life better for my customers and staff? How can I apply this idea to my organization?"

Most of the information you need is only a click away.

Essential Activity #101

Start a system to capture ideas, articles, ads, or stories that you can apply to your camps. Consider these four formats:

- An electronic file for emails, blog postings, website articles, etc.

- A paper file folder for hard copies of articles, book reviews, handwritten notes, etc.

- A box for three-dimensional mailings, audio- or videotapes, promotional products, books, and other bulky items.

- An idea journal where you can jot down ideas as they pop into your mind. If you wait until later to note your idea, chances are you won't be able to remember, so it's a good idea to carry your idea journal at all times.

Resources

One of the best ways to find information about a particular business or profession is to contact the respective trade association. They publish newsletters, magazines, online articles, research, blogs, and books related to every area of marketing.

- The Advertising Council—www.adcouncil.org

- Advertising Educational Foundation (AEF)—www.aef.com

- Advertising Research Foundation (ARF)—www.thearf.org

- Agricultural Publishers Association (APF)—www.agpub.org

- American Advertising Federation (AAF)—www.aaf.org

- Association of Business Media Companies (ABM)—www.americanbusinessmedia.com

- American Library Association (ALA)—www.ala.org

- American Marketing Association (AMA)—www.marketingpower.com

- Association for Interactive Marketing (AIM)—www.interactivehq.org

- Association of Directory Marketing (ADM)—www.admworks.org

- Association of Directory Publishers (ADP)—www.adp.org

- Association of Independent Commercial Producers (AICP)—www.aicp.com

- Association of Public Television Stations (APTS)—www.apts.org

- Association of National Advertisers (ANA)—www.ana.net

- Audit Bureau of Circulations (ABC)—www.accessabc.com

- Business Marketing Association—www.marketing.org

- Business Publications Audit of Circulation, Inc. (BPA)—www.bpaww.com

- Cable & Telecommunications Marketing Association (CTAM)—www.ctam.com

- Cable Television Advertising Bureau (CAB)—www.ontvworld.com

- Canadian Business Press (CBP)—www.cbp.ca

- Certified Audit of Circulations (CAC)—www.certifiedaudit.com

- Direct Marketing Association (DMA)—www.the-dma.org

- International Advertising Association (IAA)—www.iaaglobal.org

- Interactive Advertising Bureau (IAB)—www.iab.net

- Magazine Publishers of America (MPA)—www.magazine.org

- Marketing Research Association (MRA)—www.mra-net.org

- National Agri-Marketing Association (NAMA)—www.nama.org

- National Association of Broadcasters (NAB)—www.nab.org

- National Cable Television Association (NCTA)—www.ncta.com

- Newspaper Association of America (NAA)—www.naa.org

- Outdoor Advertising Association of America (OAAA)—www.oaaa.org

- Promotion Marketing Association of America—www.pmalink.org

- Promotional Products Association International—www.ppai.org

- Radio Advertising Bureau (RAB)—www.rab.com

- Television Bureau of Advertising (TVB)—www.tvb.org

- Word of Mouth Marketing Association (WOMMA)—www.womma.org

- Yellow Pages Association (YPA)—www.ypassociation.org

Professional Associations Related to Camps and Recreation

- American Camp Association (ACA)—www.acacamps.org—Your link to almost all information regarding accreditation, camp-specific education, and affiliated groups and chapters. Some of the larger affiliated groups are:

  √ Association of Independent Camps (AIC)—
  http://www.acacamps.org/volunteers/aicchairs/

  √ Not-for-Profit Council and Forum (NFP)—www.acacamps.org/nfpc/

  √ Religiously Affiliated Camps Council (RAC)—http://www.acacamps.org/rac/

  √ Young Professionals—www.acacamps.org/youngpros

- National Alliance for Youth Sports (NAYS)—www.nays.org—Lists all state recreation and park associations and national partners

- National Recreation and Park Association (NRPA)—www.nrpa.org—Lists all state and regional recreation and park associations, education events, and conferences

Marketing Books

The following list is just the beginning of the great, easy-to-understand assortment of marketing books you'll find at your library and bookstore. Amazon.com is a great place to search for what's new.

- *1,001 Ways to Keep Customers Coming Back: WOW Ideas That Make Customers Happy and Will Increase Your Bottom Line*, by Donna Greiner and Theodore B. Kinni

- *1001 Ways to Market Your Services: For People Who Hate to Sell*, by Richard C Crandall

- *American Generations: Who They Are, How They Live, What They Think*, by Susan Mitchell

- *Art of Cause Marketing*, by Richard Earle

- *BAM! Benefits Activated Marketing*, by Jodi Rudick (available through www.advisorsmarketing.com; includes CD-Rom software)

- *Best Customers: Demographics of Consumer Demand*, by Cheryl Russell and Susan Mitchell.

- *But We've Always Done it That Way—How to Think Outside the Brochure. Breakthrough Ideas to Makeover Your Marketing*, by Jodi Rudick (available through www.advisorsmarketing.com; includes CD-Rom software)

- *Endless Referrals* (3rd edition), by Bob Burg

- *Enterprise One to One: Tools for Competing in the Interactive Age*, by Don Peppers and Martha Rogers

- *Getting Business to Come to You*, by Paul Edwards

- *Guerrilla Marketing Series*, by Jay Conrad Levinson

- *In Search of Excellence: Lesson from America's Best-Run Companies*, by Tom Peters and Robert Waterman

- *Marketing Your Services: For People Who Hate to Sell*, by Rick Crandall

- *Ogilvy on Advertising*, by David Ogilvy

- *Permission Marketing: Turning Strangers into Friends, and Friends into Customers*, by Seth Godin

- *Principles of Marketing* (11th edition), by Philip Kotler and Gary Armstrong

- *Relationship Marketing: Successful Strategies for the Age of the Customer*, by Regis McKenna

- *Selling the Dream: How to Promote Your Product, Company, or Ideas, and Make a Difference Using Everyday Evangelism*, by Guy Kawasaki

- *The Anatomy of Buzz: How to Create Word-of-Mouth Advertising*, by Emanual Rosen

- *The Daily Dose, Volume 2—366 MORE Days of Data, Wisdom and Trends to Inspire Enthusiasm and Support for Parks, Recreation and Leisure*, by Jodi Rudick (available through www.advisorsmarketing.com; includes CD-Rom software)

- *The One-to-One Future: Building Relationships One Customer at a Time*, by Don Peppers and Martha Rogers

- *The Secrets of Word-of-Mouth Advertising*, by George Silverman

- *The Tipping Point: How Little Things Can Make a Big Difference*, by Malcom Gladwell

- *Thriving on Chaos: Handbook for a Management Revolution*, by Tom Peters

- *Unleashing the Ideavirus*, by Seth Godin

- *Why We Buy*, by Paco Underhill

- *Wise Up To Teens: Insights into Marketing and Advertising to Teenagers*, by Peter Zollo

Market Research and Demographics

The following list represents a small sampling of the hundreds of well-respected and sophisticated online and other databases and resources that you can use to gain valuable information to support marketing decisions. Some are free, some offer free trails, and some require subscriptions. Most importantly, however, is that many are accessible through library databases. Your local research librarian and the American

Library Association are great places to begin your search for research related to any area of marketing.

- Advertising World—http://advertising.utexas.edu/world—Created by the University of Texas Advertising Resource Center, this site provides an extensive collection of advertising-related links arranged alphabetically.

- American Demographics Magazine—http://www.americandemographics.com

- Annual Retail Trade Survey (U.S. Census Bureau.) Annual—Produced by the Bureau of Labor Statistics—http://www.bls.gov

- Best of the Best Home Page: Advertising and Marketing—www.ala.org—Created by members of the American Library Association, this site provides an extensive collection of marketing research sources

- Census Homepage—http://www.census.gov

- Market Guide, Published by Editor and Publisher—Produced by the "oldest journal covering the newspaper industry," this guide offers profiles, community resources, retail outlets, demographics, and other information about selected large and small cities—www.editorandpublisher.com

- Consumer Expenditure Survey, U.S. Bureau of Labor Statistics—www.bls.gov/csxhome.htm

- Dismal Scientist—www.dismalscientist.com

- Gale Directory of Publications and Broadcast Media—www.gale.com—Volumes 1 and 2 contain print and broadcast media arranged by state and city. Volume 3 provides industry statistics; lists of networks, syndicates, and publishers; and indexes of the publications by subjects, ethnicity, and formats. Volume 4 lists the sources by regional markets. Formerly the Ayer Directory of Publications.

- Geographic Information System (GIS) lets the user visualize and analyze geographic data using maps. The user can take any geography-based database and layer the different attributes on an area to do retail trade area analysis, site selection, media targeting, and much more. This process can show relationships and patterns in data better than tables, graphs, or charts. For simple GIS maps For simple GIS maps using government data, visit www.gis.com or www.factfinder.census.gov

- Household Spending: Who Spends How Much On What HC 110.C6 H68—http://stats.bls.gov—This content is based on the Bureau of Labor Statistics' annual Consumer Expenditure Survey

- Lifestyle Market Analyst, Standard Rate and Data Service—www.srds.com

- MediaMark Reporter, Annual—http://www.mediamark.com/

- Regional Economic Projections Series, NPA Data Services, Annual—http://www.npadata.com

- The Center for Public Integrity—www.publicintegrity.org —Search by zip code to find out who owns what media in your community.

- Right Site—http://www.easidemographics.com—This site offers free demographic analysis and selected "quality of life" information for specific localities.

- Sample marketing plans—http://www.bplans.com/sp/index.cfm?a=mc—These samples were created by Marketing Plan Pro.

- Seasons of Business: The Marketer's Guide to Consumer Behavior—This sources explains consumer trends for every month of the year. Trends such as business travel in August, credit cards in November, Super Bowl in January, spring break in March, and marriage in June are all explained.

About the Author

Jodi Rudick is the owner of Advisors Marketing Group, where she has worked with thousands of clients, ranging from Fortune 500 corporations to budding entrepreneurs.

Rudick began her marketing career at the age of seven, when she and her brother set off with a little red wagon going door-to-door selling imprinted Christmas and Hanukkah cards to neighbors, friends, and relatives. Since then, Rudick has sold everything from shoes and towels to sponsorships and park-development projects.

For the past 15 years, Rudick has worked exclusively in the parks, recreation, and youth-development fields. As a professional speaker and trainer, Jodi has wowed more than 1400 audiences around the globe with her endless energy, enthusiastic passion, and unique ideas. This book is Rudick's sixth title related to marketing and publicity.

Contact Jodi anytime to learn more about how to bring her high-energy workshops and programs to your staff, organization, or group. Reach her at jodi@advisorsmarketing.com or 760-809-3231.

Also by the Author

The following titles are available through www.advisorsmarketing.com:

- *BAM! Benefits Activated Marketing*

- *But We've Always Done it That Way—How to Think Outside the Brochure. Breakthrough Ideas to Make Over Your Marketing*

- *The Daily Dose, Volume 2—366 MORE Days of Data, Wisdom and Trends to Inspire Enthusiasm and Support for Parks, Recreation and Leisure*

Note: All of the above books include accompanying CD-Rom software.